no place like home

tips & techniques for real family-friendly
home design

no place like home

tips & techniques for real family-friendly home design

stephen saint-onge

Wiley Publishing, Inc.

Acquisitions Editor
Pam Mourouzis

Development Editor
Vicki Ingham

Copy Editor
Lynn Northrup

Senior Project Editor
Donna Wright

Editorial Manager
Christina Stambaugh

Vice President and Publisher
Cindy Kitchel

Vice President and Executive Publisher
Kathy Nebenhaus

Interior Design
Elizabeth Brooks

Graphics
Brent Savage

Cover Design
Wendy Mount

no place like home

For general information on our other products and services or to obtain technical support please contact our Customer Care Department within the U.S. at (877) 762-2974, outside the U.S. at (317) 572-3993 or fax (317) 572-4002.

Wiley also publishes its books in a variety of electronic formats. Some content that appears in print may not be available in electronic books. For more information about Wiley products, please visit our web site at www.wiley.com.

Library of Congress Cataloging-in-Publication Data

Saint-Onge, Stephen.
  No place like home : tips & techniques for real family-friendly home design / Stephen Saint-Onge.
    p. cm.
ISBN 978-0-470-58577-1 (pbk.)
ISBN 978-0-470-88130-9 (ebk)
  1. Interior decoration. I. Title.
  NK2115.S23 2010
  747—dc22
          2010028556
Printed in the United States of America

10 9 8 7 6 5 4 3 2 1

Book production by Wiley Publishing, Inc., Composition Services

Note to the Readers: Due to differing conditions, tools and the individual skills, John Wiley & Sons, Inc. assumes no responsibility for any damages, injuries suffered, or losses incurred as a result of following the information published in this book. Before beginning any project, review the instructions carefully, and if any doubts or questions remain, consult local experts or authorities. Because codes and regulations vary greatly, you always should check with authorities to ensure that your project complies with all applicable local codes and regulations. Always read and observe all of the safety precautions provided by manufacturers of any tools, equipment, or supplies, and follow all accepted safety procedures.

Contents

Introduction

I have always viewed the world around me as if it were a film. I tend to look at things as if seeing them through the lens of a movie camera, and I am always looking for those moments that catch my eye and draw me in. These moments are simple things that have great visual impact even though they may last only a few minutes: a child playing in the rain . . . friends gathered for dinner around a long table . . . a room lit by firelight after a cold storm settles in outside . . . the way leaves turn back-side up before a heavy rain . . . the stillness in the house after your child goes off to school. All of these cues serve to inspire me in my everyday work as a designer and as a person trying to live a good, well-rounded, creative life with my family.

Movies as Creative Muse

Film has always been a creative tool in my work, but even before I began working, film was a major influence in my life. I recall being eight years old, sitting with a pillow propped up on my lap, big sketch book in hand and a pen ready to draw a floor plan of a house in a movie I was watching on television. Most of the films that I was drawn to were old black-and-white films from the 1940s. I would draw the room that was shown on camera, but my imagination would run wild as to what rooms might lie beyond, just behind closed doors and around the corner beyond the camera's eye. I would make intricate, detailed sketches of furniture placement, of how the room might look from different camera angles, and of the outdoor spaces beyond the doors and windows of the sets. I would even go so far as to place symbols that represented the characters in the story and how they would move about that room or live in this world I was creating for them. It was very much an imaginary world that I dove into, never knowing it would help set the stage for my life's work as an adult. All of this attention to detail has helped me in my work today on photo shoots and film shoots.

I distinctly remember noticing the details of the houses in those old films. Many of the movies were set in American cities and villages, so these homes became for me a representation of American home life or what Hollywood imagined American home life to be. I suppose I was educating myself as a designer even then, and I still find myself drawn into the homes in films today because they carry me into a new world. For example, when I saw *Out of Africa* in 1985,

the house, the colors, and the mood of that film really inspired me as an artist. I realized how creating a mood is such a big part of what home is. To this day, movies remain a creative touchstone to guide me.

In movies, the mood or feeling of home is created with lighting, stylishly designed interiors, and camera angles that invite you into spaces. You can also get a sense of what the character's life is like in that setting, and the set design helps transport you to another time and place. That is what makes going to the movies so magical—you can walk in feeling one way and walk out feeling motivated, inspired, or just plain happy. I have learned over the years that our homes do that for us too.

I remember seeing Alfred Hitchcock's classic 1939 film *Rebecca*, when I was about 12 years old. It depicts the story of a young woman who marries a wealthy Englishman and moves to his family's ancestral manor house on the coast of England. Although the film was in black and

white, it had such a great mood. I could imagine myself walking around that house and feeling the sense of history in each space and the grandeur of it all, which was so different from my own life. I could almost imagine the smells in that old house, of smoldering fires in the fireplaces and the faint, lingering scent of the sea beyond.

After seeing that movie, I put masking tape on the windows of my room to create the look of leaded glass windows like those of the library I had seen in the film. I put an old velvet rug over my desk and stacked it with vintage books and old family photos to create the feeling of an ancestral library in a house somewhere in England. But to make the transformation complete, to have all my senses affected as I entered the room, I took linen writing paper and burned it in a pot from the kitchen. The smell it gave off was like the smell of a lingering fire in some ancient fireplace. It was fun and certainly sparked my imagination, because I was no longer in my small suburban bedroom.

Small Town Life

I absorbed mood, the essence of home, good design, and style from movies, but I also learned about all of these things from the people around me. The town I grew up in was very much like something in the movies—it had a diner, mom and pop stores, a market that had been there for decades, a library, a cemetery, and churches. There was a classic Texaco station and a train station that connected the quiet, idyllic life of New England to the fast-paced life of New York City. My family was the youngest in a neighborhood where people had lived in the same houses for several generations, and the neighbors became my surrogate grandparents. The houses were classic New England style. Many were white clapboard with front porches or screened-in back porches. Picket fences enclosed front lawns shaded by large maple trees or weeping willows. There always seemed to be an American flag waving in the breeze. I would walk home from school past all the houses and imagine being on the back lot of the old movie studios in Hollywood, with Teresa Wright daydreaming on her porch or Jimmy Stewart walking home from town, hearing the distant call of the train whistle in *It's a Wonderful Life*. I almost felt as if I lived in Bedford Falls when I would reach my tree-lined street. I would drop my school bag at home, greet my mom, and immediately head over to see Mrs. Blanchard, the widow in her seventies who lived across the street from my parents.

I vividly recall running through the screen door into her living room and beyond through the dining room, rooms that had been untouched by decades yet were classic in

My first photograph of my old friend (above); the house I used to visit everyday after school (below).

their design and style. I'd find her, always in a dress and apron, baking something in her kitchen—usually pies—big band music playing on the radio, curtains blowing from the open windows looking out onto her vegetable garden beyond the screened porch. It was very Norman Rockwell.

There was simplicity to life in Mrs. Blanchard's home and to her no-nonsense style. No fuss, no extra stuff, no rooms that were overly decorated, but spaces that made you feel at home just the same. In many ways, her home reminded me of the house where Teresa Wright lived in *Shadow of a Doubt*: classic, clean, and practical. No wonder that would end up being my personal design style—I was living and breathing it early on. In Mrs. Blanchard's house, the 1940s never ended. The overstuffed furniture, the vintage wallpaper, the family antiques, the bulky fridge in the kitchen near the oversized farmhouse sink, the big furnace in the center of the living room where an old black rocking chair was placed—all of these things were practical and had served her family well. It wasn't about keeping up with the Joneses or having what was trendy, but simply living a good life and doing good work.

I would spend hours in the winter in that black wicker rocker warmed by the heat of that furnace. I was told I used to do that as far back as when I was three or four years old. I would sit there for hours with Mrs. Blanchard, talking. We would share a pie, I would help around the house with chores, and as I got older, I would mow her lawn or shovel the walkway. Then inevitably I would fall asleep in that old chair. It has been decades now since Mrs. Blanchard died, and that old chair is now in my own home. I sit with my children and share with them the old movies that I still love.

In gathering information for this book, I came across a photograph (see page vii) that I took of Mrs. Blanchard the year before she died. I was about 15 years old. It was my first attempt at photography, but I felt compelled to document that moment in time, not knowing how much

the photos would come to mean to me. Now when I look at it, I am instantly transported back to what that home felt like, and I recall the old blue sweater she always had around her shoulders.

Her home was not perfect, and that was what made it feel real and comfortable. None of the houses around us were manicured or designed with a certain style or theme in mind. They were practical, they were inviting and warm, they were functional, and they were as individual as the people who inhabited them. That is what home truly is—not someone else's idea of what home should be, but your own.

I am married now with a family of my own. Yes, I live in a white clapboard farmhouse with rocking chairs on the porch. Maple trees and a picket fence are nearby, and Mrs. Blanchard's old flag hangs off my house. As I write this, I think about how my greatest joys in life are focused around my home. In summer, I love mowing my lawn. I enjoy checking that off my to-do list, but what I love most is walking around my house after finishing the job. At dusk, the lights of my home glow and I see my family inside going about their business. I think how simple this sight is, and yet it truly is what life is all about: home and family. As my children grow up, I see how we imprint our homes with our personal histories and journeys, and I see now, more than ever, what my home gives back to me. Memories are made there—simple, fun, crazy, moving, cinematic moments that we act out in the setting of our homes.

Me with some of the kids in Africa

A Career in Design

My days on that tree-lined street led me to become a creative artist who wears many hats. I worked in film and television and eventually designed for private clients. The work brought success and accolades for which I am very grateful. Some of my projects came to the attention of the media, and that began my journey of designing on television for various programs in front of millions of people. Then came opportunities to write and design for home magazines and newspapers across the country and to be a spokesperson for the all-American family home and family-focused lifestyle. But I'm still just the guy who loves doing design. Part of me will always be that kid sitting in the old rocking chair watching movies. When I talk about design and lifestyle, I'm speaking from the heart.

At first, doing design was all about creating a space that worked well. But as the years have gone by, it has become more of a mission—to help uplift people with design and to open their eyes to what their environments can do for them. I recently traveled to Africa with my wife to start an art program for orphans. It was probably one of the most amazing experiences of our lives. Here were young people who had nothing. No family. No home. Although many had been raised since they were infants in a cold, uninviting orphanage, they had joy. Many were already self-taught artists, and they created in the midst of so much adversity. I was overcome by their openness and sense of hope. Their imaginations and creativity saved them. The artwork that they produced was magical. We were all excited about what we were starting, but it also made us realize how lucky we are.

Coming back to my house after the trip, I walked around it with new eyes. I have a new vantage point not only on what my home means to me and how good life is here in America, but also about what I want my creative work to do,

"It's about simply living a good life and doing good work."

whether it is in design, in film, in television, or in connecting with other people in a real way. Simply put, I want to encourage you to live your best life, to do all that you can personally and as a family to affect other lives and the life of your community in good ways. Where does home come into this? It's the incubator, the foundation, the haven—the safe place that nurtures you and equips you to go off and do the best work of your life every day.

When I began thinking about how to share with you what I do as a designer and how I do it, I realized that much of what I would be doing is showing you rather than telling you. This is why I was inspired to take my own photographs of real-life homes, capturing real people and how they live. This way I could illustrate to you what I notice, what stands out to me, and what inspires me—and how I translate that into home design. Being a painter as well as a designer, I am inspired by the lines, color, and light in a room, and sometimes I feel the mood or essence can be conveyed better with art than with photographs. So you'll see some of my paintings in here, too.

My goal for this book is to be like a friend talking to you about home and design rather than a designer telling you what to do. Good home design is not a mystery; it is not unattainable. I want to inspire you to be excited about your home again.

As I have gone to families' homes around the country to photograph the images for this book, I am humbled by the fact that people have allowed me to witness their lives and environments. Some of the homes are my designs; some were designed by the homeowners themselves. I hope that by the time you finish reading this book, you will have the inspiration and creative tools to make your own home truly yours— so that, as the last line in *The Wizard of Oz* says, you too can say, "There's no place like home."

Part I

Getting Started

chapter 1

Beginning

People often tell me they don't know how to figure out what their style is—and that they don't have time to figure it out. They're too busy taking the kids to hockey practice or ballet classes, and they're on the PTA. As a father I can fully understand that time seems to fly by, and sometimes the way your house looks is the last thing on your mind. However, there comes a moment when you realize that your home does affect your life and that you deserve to make both of them better.

To help you start your design plan, let me share a few things that I know from experience. First off, you do not have to give your own personal style a label. For some homeowners, identifying with a particular style makes choices easier and gives them confidence. That alone can be empowering and motivating. However, I have seen wonderful homes that fit no particular style category but reflect an evolution of sorts, creating an environment that truly represents the people who live there. That's the real goal of home design: taking who you are, where you have been, where you want to go, and what you have to work with now, and sculpting a style that is all your own.

There is nothing wrong with mimicking rooms that you see in furniture catalogs, but you have to see yourself living in those spaces—so you need to personalize the look to your lifestyle. Yes, you can have the key pieces of living room furniture from "X" store, but you need to create a room around it and bring in finishing details that say it is yours. That is part of what the journey of this book is about—helping you see design in a new, attainable, and approachable way.

> There is nothing more exciting and uplifting than being able to say "I created that!"

Second, some homeowners feel that they must buy everything that is trendy or hot right now or "in style." My advice is that it's better to keep your home style flexible, because your tastes will change. Having a basic knowledge of your style will simplify your life and make putting a room together easier. You can begin with that style identity and then evolve and grow. Bottom line: You already have the power within you to make your home come to life. Believe me, there is nothing more exciting and uplifting than being able to say "I created that!"

Third, it's important to stay focused. If you begin a project and don't finish it, that drains you emotionally and will keep your home from being a place that restores and energizes you. To avoid that, set attainable goals. Whether you embark on a small design change or a bigger renovation, if you stay on track and meet your goals, you will feel better. Accomplishing what you set out to do is a great boost to your morale!

Another thing I have learned over the years as a designer is that it's important to follow your instincts—listen to your intuition or your inner voice when you're making choices. Your first impression of something is usually the way to go.

> Stay focused and set attainable goals. Accomplishing what you set out to do is a great boost to your morale!

When you start doubting yourself or listening to everyone else, you lose sight of what you initially felt good about. Just as in other areas of life, quieting your mind to get in tune with your inner voice can help clarify your thinking about home design. If you feel overwhelmed by the decisions ahead of you, calm down and keep reading.

When I started doing makeovers on television, the schedule was hectic and I usually had to design several rooms for different episodes at the same time, working only from a videotape the field producer would send me from homes across the country. Usually I would have a few hours to design the room, without ever meeting the owners or seeing the room in person. I loved that challenge and loved being creative on my feet. One of my favorite quotes reads something like this: "Being faced with limitations or limited resources forces artists to be their most creative . . . and from that comes their best work." In a short amount of time, I would do sketches and come up with a product list and an overall plan for the whole makeover. There was no time to second-guess myself. When I saw the befores, images of the afters would instantly come to mind, and I learned over time that I should stick to my original gut reaction of what to do.

In the process of designing that way, I would ask myself, *What are the homeowners saying (in the videotape) that is capturing the essence of what the room should be? What is the emotional nugget of what the room deserves to be for those particular people?* This is the listening part of design. It's part of the interpreting process. Imagine the large piece of raw marble that Michelangelo faced when he began a new work of art. It's all about chipping away to see what's in there.

In preparing for the television makeovers, I learned to be quick in my creative decisions. Once the design plan was set into motion with sketches, building details and projects, and focal points, I would have conference calls with the producers, the director, and other talent involved in the project. This is usually the same process for my magazine projects, too. My initial vision takes form and develops a life of its own that is not just in my mind anymore. It is my job to keep that vision clear from conception through execution, backtracking from the vision to the starting point. You can do this, too.

It's not about perfection. If it feels right to you—go with it. If it feels wrong or if you are having doubts—move on. But in that process, if you make mistakes or if small things do not go as planned, that's okay, too. Out of the mistakes or small dramas come opportunities for something unexpected that may be even better than what you had planned. For example, say you are renovating and you had your heart set on opening up the wall, but you can't because of plumbing lines. So you start looking at other options and realize that a doorway makes more sense. You haven't strayed from your original plan too much; you have learned to be creative on your feet.

With all of my makeovers, I knew I had hit the nail on the head if I made an emotional connection with the owner. That nugget or emotional charge is what I wanted to get right. It could be a theme for the room, a bunch of photographs on display, or even just the essence of what the room stands for. If I saw in the homeowner's eyes when they walked in that they connected (with tears was always great!), that was everything. It was always a thrill seeing that original vision come to life.

Environmental Awareness

How do you learn to see your environment and understand how it affects—or reflects—you? Here's the first trick: Put yourself in my shoes as you walk into your own home.

Imagine me walking through your front door for the first time. What would I see first in your hall? What would I see as I looked from the front door into the room beyond? Would I notice clutter? Would I notice your nice collection of artwork? Would I be drawn into the room by an inviting seating area? Would I notice the roaring fire in your living room fireplace? Would you find yourself saying things like "Don't look at that wall, it was painted by the previous owner" or "I hate this furniture, but we spent a lot of money on it and are just making it work for now," or "My husband's recliner is not supposed to be in here . . . but it's too bulky in the family room"? If you listen to your instincts, you know when a piece of furniture doesn't blend in, the pictures are hung too high, or the style of the room doesn't really reflect who you are.

Start noticing things about your rooms that work or don't work. What do you see as good and bad, the positives and the negatives? Your goal is not to see all that is wrong about a room, but rather see the good and celebrate it. Take what is not working and make a change in

*Give yourself a good environment to live in now

the right direction. Don't worry about your home not being perfect. *It will change as you change.* Besides, you do not have to put off having your dream home down the road—have it now, but just call it your dream home in progress. Make what you have now work for you now. Life is short. Give yourself a good environment to live in now.

I'll give you an example of what not to do. I knew a couple who lived and worked for years in a small, one-room urban apartment. Whenever I walked in there I felt depressed. It was just a place to drop off things and sleep. For dinner or fun, they had to go out. It was lifeless inside, and there was no light—literally and figuratively. It housed a mishmash of furniture, no inviting seating areas, no sofa, no artwork. Especially in a city environment, you need to have a haven, a place to recharge, and this place was far from that. It would have taken so little to change it—a can of paint for some warm color on the walls, a sofa bed to double as sleeping and seating, and some lighting to brighten it all up.

Another example, a positive one: I did a television makeover a few years back for a woman and her family. I was asked to do a major renovation of the main part of the house in three weeks. Through the magic of television it moved smoothly, and it's probably one of my favorite projects because it truly was part of the process of my learning to trust my instincts.

I walked into this suburban home and immediately thought that it didn't fit this young, vibrant mom. It felt like someone else's idea of a home—her mother's, perhaps? In fact, many of the pieces had come from her mother. In talking with her for about an hour, I learned that she and

her family never used their adjoining living room and dining room because she grew up in a house where those rooms were only used at holiday times or on special occasions. So these rooms in her own home were formal and far from family-friendly. My immediate thought was, *Why put off living in and using those rooms every day?* The

This is one of my favorite TV makeover projects.

family walked through those rooms daily, but they never stopped to enjoy them. All of that changed after the three-week makeover/renovation.

After the renovation, the house felt more like a vacation home. It was very family-friendly, warm, and comfortable. The rooms could now be used for family and friends to gather in. When the homeowner walked through the renovated house for the first time, she saw her whole house from a new perspective. It was thrilling, because I could see what an emotional difference this made. The makeover began a whole new chapter in that family's life. Same house, new perspective.

Learning to See

To start learning to see your home with new eyes, choose a time when you are rested, not hungry or distracted by family or deadlines. Walk through each room of your home, sit down, and just look around. Notice what works or doesn't work. I want you to start noticing the details—simple as that. I want you to learn to see what is around you or what you have chosen to surround yourself with. Ask yourself the following questions as you enter each room. Write down your answers in quick bullet-point form if you like, but just *notice* things for now. Get your family members to do the same exercise, and compile all the answers when you're finished.

- When I walk through the front door of my home, what do I notice first? It could be a bad banister, a bright paint color, an inviting table with family photos, or even a clean view into another room.

- When I walk through my kitchen door or other entrance, what do I notice first? Maybe a well-organized kitchen, the smell of fine cooking, or an inviting gathering place by a fireplace.

- Does the first impression this house makes on others represent me or not? When friends come to visit, what is my house saying about me? That I am rushed and living a chaotic life or that I have a home that is vibrant and in balance?

*A well-organized kitchen is inviting

*Storage keeps a mudroom organized

Great natural light

- What is the first view I have as I enter each room, from various entrances? Maybe it's artwork on one wall, new drapes, a buckling floor or chipped plaster.

- Is this my dream home or room? If not, could it be, under all this stuff?

- What do I like most about this room and why?

- What do I like least about this room and why?

- What in each room is a must-keep? Look at everything from furniture to accessories and see if it works. If not, could it be donated, sold, or repurposed somewhere else?

- What is the lighting like in the room? Is there natural light? Is there good interior lighting? Lighting can affect any design in a good or bad way.

- How are all my senses affected when I enter? Does the house smell good? How do the colors and light levels make me feel? What do I hear?

- Do I enjoy coming home at the end of the day?

- What would I like my house to say about me and my family?

Defining Your Style

The answers to this room inventory are the first stage in your journey of making your house a home. To help you take the next step, start to zero in on the style or look that captures who you really are. Here are some basic style categories and their characteristics. Do any of them speak to you?

Country House/Rural Style

- Warm, inviting, and lived in.

- You might like taking a fall foliage trip to Vermont in October and driving past white clapboard farmhouses, staying at welcoming and cozy bed-and-breakfast places in Maine, and rummaging through architectural salvage shops in search of a distressed mantel or old doors you can reuse in your newly built home. You appreciate the finest of the old, but love mixing it with some new pieces to create a look that is vintage, distressed, and rustic.

- You like things that have some character and are a bit more lived in. You like a house or pieces with history. You enjoy mixing fabrics—maybe stripes with faded floral slipcovers—or worn leather sofas, and using vintage store signs as artwork on the walls.

- You want to recapture those inviting places that might have been at your favorite getaway. Maybe it's that beach house in a film you saw (*Something's Gotta Give* with Diane Keaton, for example) or a quiet English cottage with a roaring fire as the room's focal point (think *Howards End* from Merchant Ivory). Those are both very country in style—yet one is twenty-first-century country style and the other is nineteenth century and period in style.

- For some people, themed wallpaper borders or stencils capture country style. Though not my favorite way of expressing what country style is, it works for some people, and that is fine, too.

- You walk into this style of home, and you feel *at ease*. You feel welcomed into it, and you want to linger for awhile. It's not your grandmother's house, but there is something familiar about it.

Accessories, ladderback chairs, and bin-style cabinet pulls say country style.

- You may have a new house that is basic in detail, yet you choose slipcovered fabrics, distressed wood furniture, a vintage mantelpiece for your fireplace, and a farmhouse table in your dining room. Maybe you even opt for open shelving in your new kitchen to display your collection of vintage china and cookware. This can bring you into the country-style category without having a stenciled border or duck in sight!

I remember looking at a house years ago that was for sale. It was being run as a bed-and-breakfast and had room after room filled with antiques. I walked through the rooms trying to envision them with my own things in them and came away with two images: the smoldering fire in the oversized period fireplace in the large living room and the screened doors on the entrances. The doors were open, welcoming and inviting. That was the essence of that country house to me.

Period houses can also convey the essence of what I see as country style. I grew up going to the Shelburne Museum in Vermont. This unique complex was assembled by the Webb family and includes 25 historic structures that were dismantled, moved to the site, and rebuilt. The buildings and exhibition spaces display American artwork, vintage toy collections, vintage clothing, quilts, and artifacts. When you walk into the rebuilt historical homes, you step back in time. The houses are set up just as they would have been in 1620, 1860, or 1900. I admire people who buy vintage homes and preserve them as they once were. They re-create the time period of those homes not only in how they renovate them, but also in how they furnish them, down to the last detail, maintaining the essence of the period while making the house work for everyday, modern living.

*Graphic pattern and modern chairs say urban style

City House/Urban Style

- No clutter, clean lines, and simple.
- You have—or dream of—a place in New York City, Miami, Malibu, or Chicago that's clutter-free with clean lines and modern furniture. Maybe it's all black and white in a very dramatic style: white walls with classic, oversized black-and-white photography framed in black with large white mats, sleek black leather furniture and very few accessories. You might like showing off your streamlined technology, such as a flat-screen TV mounted on the wall or the latest in sound systems. You might have dramatic displays of a favorite collection (books, pottery, art, vintage oil cans), or you might have a distinct 1940s theme with a masculine undertone to it.

- This style is uncluttered. Everything serves a purpose, and the spaces feel open, well-organized, and functional. You walk in feeling that all is in order, and you can focus on any task at hand with great purpose and efficiency.

- You like using open space to lead the eye to something dramatic—such as a stripped-down seating area with just a sofa, a chair, and a table with a simple bowl of fruit on it. You might use lighting to draw the eye toward a long wall of vibrant, oversized artwork. You find the rawness of industrial spaces appealing—exposed pipes and rough brick or concrete like you'd find in a city loft. You like making a statement in a clean and sharp-looking way.

- You are not afraid of color or lack of color. You may have one dramatic red wall that really catches your eye when you walk in, and that is the only color in the whole room. Or you like the serene calm of no color, such as white on white, so when you look at the room, it is visually spare and minimalist.

Classic House/Traditional Style

- Inviting, can be formal, and what I think of as the "typical" American family home.

- You are not into being trendy or keeping up with fashions. To you it is more about sustained style because you have made classic choices in your furniture that will stand the test of time. The pieces will be there for a while. Think of fashion: The basic black dress for women and the basic navy blue suit or sport coat for men never go out of style, but you can always update them with the latest accessories. The same applies to classic home design.

- There are probably pieces that are antique, maybe handed down from your parents or grandparents, in your home. Maybe your formal mahogany dining room table is a piece you grew up with. Traditional style has a hint of formality. It can still be inviting, but it remains classic and in some cases, safe. Safe because it is what your mom did or what your neighbors do.

- The house that I think of as typically traditional is the house in *Father of the Bride* (the remake with Diane Keaton and Steve Martin). The Colonial-style house in that movie is classic inside and out—symmetrical, with double-hung windows and shutters, wide door frames, and wainscoting. I fell in love with that set because for me it captured the traditional American family home. It is formal, yet you could easily live there. Depending on where you live, however, your idea of traditional may reflect a different architectural or cultural heritage— Spanish colonial or Craftsman bungalow, for example. If your decorating choices reflect that heritage, you can consider yourself a traditionalist.

*Furniture based on historic styles creates a classic look

Eclectic Home/Mixing It Up

- Not afraid of risk-taking in design, well-traveled, artistic, and definitely wanting to express yourself.

- You like mixing things together and are confident in doing so. Maybe you boldly mix fabric styles or wall colors. You might have collections of things from your travels that you show off in interesting ways. Your spaces are unique and not re-creations from a catalog. You have defined who you are in these spaces. They truly reflect you and your family with the vivid mix of things and how they are all brought together.

- You are not afraid of layering. You like old and new, but you like things that tell a story or remind you of places you have been.

*Mix styles for an eclectic look

This style is different from country because of the wide-ranging mix of influences—exotic, primitive, modern, and high-style period pieces can all work together. It may even be a bit more cluttered than country style. The details are layered. I think of artists' studios or of that camp in the film *On Golden Pond*—places that capture moments in time from your family history, your life, and what you care about. The home in the 2007 film *Dan in Real Life* has that feel, too. It can be a place that stands still in time or a place that is full of life from what is going on around you right now.

Clarify Your Style Identity

It's fine to have a little of each style in your personal style file. You may find that you like a little of each, and that's okay. To help you further zero in on your favorite style, notice ads in magazines and rooms on television shows. Pay attention to the ones that particularly appeal to you and see if you can match them up with the previous style descriptions. This can help guide you toward the style you're most likely to enjoy living with.

Here is another way to get at defining your style. It can be a fun exercise to do with friends and family, and it is useful to see what others have to say about your present rooms and home. In the final analysis, always listen to yourself first to determine what you intend or want to do with your spaces, but use their input to your advantage now.

- Have them look at your current room now (the one you want to redesign) and pick out two or three things that they think make you lean toward a certain style. For example, maybe your sofa screams country, or maybe it is very modern. Maybe you have a collection of teapots in your kitchen, or you have framed your family photos in a distinct way that leans toward an urban look.

- How would these people describe you? Do you have a certain style in your appearance and the way you dress that's also reflected in your home? For example, if you

have a fresh, modern haircut and you dress and present yourself in an energetic, youthful style, does your home reflect that or do you seem out of your element?

- What do they love about your home now and why?

- What doesn't work for them and why?

- Ask your friends if they can remember what they imagined your home to be like before they knew you well or had seen your house. Was it what they expected when they finally came over?

Defining your style helps guide you toward a clearer sense of who you are in your home. Once you know that, making decisions about how to bring your rooms together will be easier and more enjoyable because you will have that style touchstone for creative direction. A sense of your style identity doesn't give you a blueprint for exactly how to proceed, but rather a framework to guide you in the right direction. That's not to say that you have to wear blinders and be single-minded. So for now, stay focused on a particular style that best fits you and keep moving forward with confidence. This limits the chaos and confusion. You want to keep things simple. It may not be brain surgery, but details matter, and that requires focus.

Here is a good place to ask how your choice *feels*. When you were reading the previous style options, did you automatically pick one style but hear a voice inside say, *That other style is really more me?* Did you second-guess yourself, thinking you might not be able to pull off that other style?

Go with that voice inside. As in life, you can't let fear get in your way. Move forward and see where things take you. If you make decisions based on fear or keeping things safe, you won't grow, expand, and discover new things. That vision of who you are can be different from the one everyone else sees. You know yourself and owe it to yourself to move confidently in a direction that may seem scary or that you may not be able to envision completely yet.

To move forward with confidence, you need a plan of action. In anything you do in life, you need a vision of what you want to accomplish. If you are not clear about what you want, or about your intentions, how can anyone else know, and how can it possibly come together? With a clear, well-thought-out, creative plan in hand, you can begin to construct the collage that will become your (re)designed room. I use the word "collage" because the room is built of layers of things coming together. Each layer has to be planned, whether it's for a quick turnaround project or a more involved renovation.

Go with that voice inside. As in life, you can't let fear get in your way.

What Needs Changing?

When you are ready to focus on redesigning a specific room, photos can help you see the space from a fresh perspective. The following technique can help motivate you to make change happen, even in small ways, because you will have a clearer vision of it—and that is creatively exciting.

- Take photos of your room from all angles as it is right now. You want to be able to see it for what it truly is. Here's a trick that I use: I photograph the befores of the room from the same angles that I envision the most dramatic changes taking place. For example, if I stand in the foyer and look into a living room that has a boring mantel with no detail, I know that in the after, the mantel will be transformed with detail and color that make it dramatic visually. So I take the before shot from that spot in the foyer and shoot the after from the same location. Do this, and you will be able to develop your skills of being able to *see the room as a designer sees it*.

If you are not sure what the after might look like, look for the best views into the room. Is there a wall with interesting detail? Or a doorway framing what could be a great view of a room? Is there a corner with attractive moldings and windows? Look at magazines for some ideas on how to shoot your befores and your beautiful afters. These photos are for your use as a creative tool. You don't have to share them, but somehow I think you'll be wanting to at the end of your project! Print them for reviewing later.

- Now go in and remove the clutter from all the surfaces—tabletops, shelves, and countertops. You want as blank a canvas as possible so you can see the big picture. Remove even the window treatments and everything hanging on the walls. Put the things that are must-haves or that you love in one central area. Things that you are not sure about or that you don't really need can go in another location for now. (Think out of sight, out of mind.).

- With the space emptied out, take more pictures from the same angles as before. Print these shots, too.

- Now compare the photos. Looking at your room this way is almost like looking at a magazine makeover with befores and afters. It helps you step back from a space you know so well that you no longer see it because you are too close to it. In this exercise you can consider it in a new way.

- Think about what stands out to you in the pictures. Does the wall color make the room feel dark? Do the woodwork and cabinets make the room feel dingy and closed in? Could that small window be replaced to allow in light or take advantage of a view that was hidden? Has that wallpaper seen its last day? Also look at what stands out as good. In the kitchen, your appliances may look better with all the photos and notes removed from the refrigerator and the oven mitts and cooking utensils out of sight. Maybe without the clutter on the counters, the kitchen feels more open. Maybe you want to go in a more modern direction or warm up the spaces with touches of country style. You can start to see new possibilities.

- From here, create a "punch list" (your To-Do list) of things you can do now to make what is good better and steps you can take to dramatically improve the things that are not so good. This list gives you a plan—something to start dreaming about and being creative with.

- The fun part of any makeover is looking at the before and in-process images and then seeing the final results. Seeing what you have accomplished is empowering—so remember to take pictures before, during, and after your projects!

- You might find that your space is not so bad and that simple changes will really make a difference—painting a room, adding new accessories or lighting, replacing window treatments, and so on could be all that's needed. So it could be transformed in a short amount of time. Or you could be setting the stage for longer-range goals and a small renovation. Just beginning the process sets the wheels in motion. You want to end up seeing what you have to work with.

The punch list will bring up the issue of budget. You might see that you need new furniture or new storage, so you start thinking about cost. Then you have to look again and see if you really need those things. Yes, you may want new appliances, but can the existing ones work for now? Is the floor really that bad? Are the kitchen or bathroom countertops workable? Be honest with yourself about the space. Remember, you can make any space look big-budget without actually spending a lot of money. In kitchens, for example, I like to mix ideas from chef-friendly, high-end kitchen showrooms with things I've seen in Euro-influenced, less expensive product showrooms. It's all about making what you have better, and then setting the stage to create the feeling you're going for. Making your home good for you and your family is a journey. One day you have a nursery for your baby—then a kid's room . . . a teen's room. Maybe with job promotions and a little money to spend, you decide to renovate your house. So to-do lists are always in-progress because our homes are never really done; they are environments that evolve and flow with changes in our lives. Home represents our lives and who we are.

Now it's time to begin. Your home holds great possibilities . . . so go for it! It all starts with something so simple: *Beginning . . . .*

chapter 2

Creative Tools

People often ask me, "How do I figure out what my style is?" Or they'll wonder, "How do I know I'm making the right purchases for my home? There are so many choices, and I just walk away drained, without making any decisions." The answer to the first question is that no one can tell you what your style is but you. That is part of making your home your own, by pulling together a look that is unique to you and your setting. The answer to the second question is, focus on your goal. That will help take the stress out of shopping and decision-making.

I know that can be easier said than done for many people. But I know from experience that when you figure out what you want, everything starts to fall into place. I love a statement inspired by Goethe: "Whatever you can do, or dream you can, begin it. Boldness has genius, power, and magic in it." This holds true for your home, because if you can get beyond the fear of not knowing what your style is and begin to make informed decisions, you will see things coming to life.

The Look Book

How do you figure out what you want and start making those informed decisions? For me, the answer is the *Look Book:* simple and easy—and fun. If I were sitting at your kitchen table with you now, I'd urge you to gather images from magazines or catalogs of rooms you love. I'd give you a 20-minute time frame and tell you to spread the magazines or catalogs out on the table in front of us. The time frame is just to keep the project moving quickly so you can start the process—it's all about *beginning it.*

The idea is to pull visuals of rooms or things that catch your eye and that you like—keep it simple and easy, and don't mull it over or second-guess yourself. Just respond to images, but don't try to find certain rooms or things just for the sake of finding them. See what your eyes rest on or that you go back to as you flip through the pages. If you can rip out or cut out the pages, that is even better because you can spread them on the table and start creating a montage of images.

It's also okay to add pictures of things that don't relate specifically to the home. For example, an image of an outfit you love or a vacation scene that appeals to you can give you clues to your personal style and the kind of environment you'd like to live in. It's part of the process of thinking about how you envision yourself living in your house and what your own personal style may be. Finding your personal style connects to your home style as well. It's an extension of you. How many times have you seen someone who has a great personal look and you wonder what his or her house might be like? Do you think her style might be a perfect fit for the way she lives in her home each day?

The images in front of you start to form a picture of what you like or are drawn to. This is the beginning of the creative process of finding *you* in there. If I were sitting with you, I might ask you a few questions:

- What do you like about the room images you chose?
- When you look at those images, what feeling do you get?
- What is it about each room that you first noticed? Paint color, furniture style, layout?
- Is the room an example of what your dream home might be?
- If it *is* dream home material, what can you take away from that dream room and re-create in your home now?

Ask yourself the same questions about all of the images you gathered. You can even use a pen and mark up the images to remind yourself what you loved in each.

- Now, from a personal style standpoint, if you have an outfit you love, what do you like about it?
- What does the style or look say to you? Is it creative? Eclectic? Traditional? Classic? Modern?
- Is it you the way you see yourself now or is it how you might like to see yourself change?

The idea of using vision boards at home or at work has become popular as a way of making good things happen. It is believed that if you spend time looking at images of places or things you love and giving them attention once a day or so, you will eventually draw those things into your life. In a way, the Look Book idea is like that, because once you gather images of things you love in one place, you can focus your attention on them to start making things happen.

The Look Book is a sort of bible of your home or the way you want your home to be. It is important to say that the Look Book concept came from my wife, Mary. Early on

*The Look Book can help couples or families mesh styles

Works of art may inspire colors that you love for your rooms.

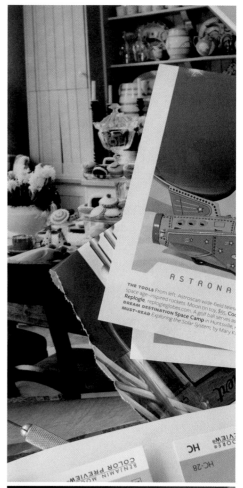

in our life together, she took a sketchbook and simply started gathering images of rooms or things she loved as she came across them. Eventually I started adding things or rooms that I liked, too. We would add notes of details we wanted to remember, paint colors we had seen and loved, and even fabric samples that caught our eye. It became a powerful tool for us as we started figuring out what our own style was as a couple and as we progressed into various homes over time. The images, which were gathered in no particular order, served as a guide as we made decisions about projects or things we wanted to buy. So we may have cut out a kitchen design we loved from a magazine and pasted it into the book, even though we were not planning a kitchen renovation at that point. Years later, when we were doing a kitchen renovation, we had the visual tools in front of us from our Look Book to remind us of what we wanted. It also became a good way for us to show each other what we wanted for a room and helped us communicate clearly with contractors and salespeople. The Look Book gave us a way to empower ourselves and move confidently in the direction of making educated decisions for our home.

I have also used the Look Book concept for my design work. I gather ideas in my design Look Book to remind me of projects or things I have seen that were interesting or creative. When I need inspiration, I flip through the pages and begin to get ideas. I might not use the exact idea or concept shown in the images, but I can take away certain elements or features and repurpose them for what I am working on. I might like the way a tabletop is styled or how colors are layered in a room or in props— or how bookcases are constructed. I might see a living room that is French in style, and down the road if I want to do a French-inspired design I can go back to it and see how certain items play a part in re-creating that look.

The Look Book is about gaining inspiration from all that is around us every day and remembering those things later.

Make Your Own Look Book

The Look Book is about gaining inspiration from all that is around us every day and remembering those things later.

To make your own Look Book, buy an artist's sketchbook or a large scrapbook that you can paste things into. I like a hardcover sketchbook because it feels more like a book. Plus, I find the three-ring binder not as appealing to handle. I want something that feels like an ancient book that I have created over time.

To add to the great feeling of this book, make a cover for it. Take an image of a dream house you love or make a collage of things about homes that make you smile. For me, it's white clapboard farmhouses, vintage pickup trucks, American flags, and houses at twilight lit from inside. Handwrite the title or print something in a font you love on your computer, and tear the edges for a more rustic look. Glue the images onto the sketchbook cover and seal them with decoupage medium. This adds a clear finish and protects the cover. You might want to do this as family with a sketchbook for each person.

Filling the pages is an ongoing process. Sit down with a pile of magazines and catalogs and start tearing out images (and be sure to recycle the magazines and catalogs once you're done—the idea is to get rid of them and get them out of the house). You might want to divide the book by categories or rooms. That makes it easier to find ideas when you're thinking about a specific project—kitchens, bedrooms, paint, storage, and so on. You don't have to be neat or perfect. I actually like the collaged look for the pages. I also like leaving room for handwritten words or notes about what you like about the rooms or things . . . just ways of marking up what you love and reminding yourself of those things later on, years from now as you return to the pages of your Look Book for guidance.

When you go to paint stores, bring home paint swatches of colors you like and paste those into your book. You might want to have a page in your book dedicated to paint colors that are in your home now as a record for future reference. Paint a sample of the color in

your book and note which room it is in and what the brand, paint name, and finish are. This makes it easier when you are trying to match furniture or accessories and also makes it easier if you need to touch up walls or trim and you have 300 different paint cans in the garage.

Inspiration Is Everywhere

Be on the lookout for inspiration everywhere—Web sites for home furnishings companies, friends' houses, show houses. Take digital pictures of your friends' homes as visual reminders of what you liked. They will no doubt be flattered that you like what they chose, but the point isn't for you to copy them but to use the pictures as idea starters and reminders. I also like to use my Look Book to add notes, sketches, and simple ideas to guide me in my projects. Sometimes I'll just write a list of ideas to remind me of things that I've seen at a house.

As time passes, your Look Book will get bulky and worn—which is good. You will find that when you go out shopping, you can take it along and know what you want to look for because the items you have gathered there and the notes that you have made are all tailored to you and what you respond to. The looks may not be one particular style, but you are beginning to define your style by bringing together things you respond to. You are beginning to look at things in a new way. You see a room in a picture—you like something about it—it resonates with you somehow. So then you begin to pick the room apart to discover what you like about it. If you like the arrangement but the furniture is not your style, note that on the photo ("I only like the seating arrangement here"). You may have a small house now, but the dining room furniture you love is shown in a big, open-plan room. That's okay—you can dream!

The Look Book can be useful for a family, or a couple, trying to mesh their styles. It can be frustrating when there are several people living in a house and everyone has different ideas of what the house should look like, or when one person has opinions and the other does not. Having a Look Book that you build together over time can unify your design direction. At the very least, it begins a conversation and helps you focus on what everyone might want. For example, the kids might want purple walls in their bedroom but as a parent you can't live with that—so you work out a compromise with purple bedding and accessories. Your husband might want that bulky recliner in a photo he found, but you want a more classic look. Talking

*Use your Look Book to communicate with salespeople or contractors when making purchases

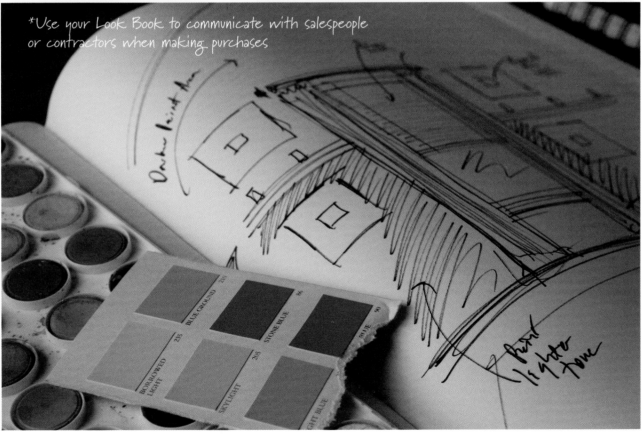

about it may reveal that the important thing for him is to be able to kick back and relax in a chair. The focus then becomes finding a recliner that looks classic in style yet offers the comfort he wants without being too bulky and big for the room.

The Look Book is a great way to communicate your point to sales staff. When you're shopping for counter-tops or appliances, open your book to pages with products you love and show those to sales staff to illustrate the look you are going for. Remember, however, if you show an image of a high-end kitchen to the salesperson, he or she will likely show you high-end appliances. If that's not in your budget, explain to the salesperson that this is the look you are going for, but you need a budget-friendly option.

Create movie magic in your own home environment

Finally, the Look Book can be invaluable when you are doing a renovation and need to meet with contractors or painters. Showing them a picture of what you want to accomplish will help them understand your goals much better than vague descriptions can. Use your book as a creative way to empower your voice as a homeowner.

Life Imitating Art: Using Films for Inspiration

Ever since I was a kid, movies resonated with me in a big way because they not only entertained me, they educated me. I learned to notice the rooms and settings and how they created a mood or environment around the

This LA kitchen from *The Holiday* is a great example of comfortable modern style.

Favorite Films for Design Ideas

Here are some of my favorite films for great homes and good design ideas.

Out of Africa: This is the house I would build if I ever built from scratch. Love the use of stone and the wide porches. Great living room with stone fireplace, too.

The Holiday: A great opportunity to look at a variety of styles, from a cozy English cottage to a modern LA house, with others in between. Look for the amazing kid's bedroom tent, too.

Practical Magic: A Victorian house with a terrific kitchen—great example of layering to create warmth and visual interest in a gathering space.

Stepmom: Early 1900s home that suits a modern family. A good example of how to create a setting that is lived in and one that you want to come home to. Love the family dancing scene, too!

Holiday Inn: A must-watch for me every year. Love the idea of a big old rambling farmhouse like this. Great use of windows, and note the open floor plan of the interior.

Father of the Bride (1991 remake with Steve Martin and Diane Keaton): Colonial Revival architecture outside, the perfect All-American home inside. The layout of the house is a perfect family-home style. Kitchen was and remains one of my favorites. The sequel (*Father of the Bride Part II*, 1995) has an amazing baby nursery.

What Lies Beneath: Contemporary lake house shot in Vermont. Beautiful exterior; interior has a great use of muted color palettes and represents a look that suits many current family lifestyles.

Howards End: The ultimate romantic country cottage. The opening scene is my favorite—seeing your home at twilight. Magic hour.

Under the Tuscan Sun: Anyone who is renovating should see this film. It just captures the essence of what home is supposed to be in the end (love the ending) and what you are working toward.

Christmas in Connecticut: True Hollywood style, but so much you can draw from. Great oversized fireplace and an amazing open-plan living room. Second to *Out of Africa*, I would build this stone house and live in it.

Shadow of a Doubt: Captures the mood of Main Street USA in the 1940s. Classic family house that reminds me of the houses I grew up around. Great porch.

Mr. Blandings Builds His Dream House: After years of looking for my own dream house, I ended up in a house that looks much like this one. Life imitating art or the other way around?

On Golden Pond: A perfect family getaway camp. A place to keep all your family memories. A place to return to every summer. I like the idea of that.

Shoot the Moon: A rambling farmhouse style.

Bringing Up Baby: Another example of what Hollywood imagined a country house should look like. Great mix of materials. Might inspire you.

Driving Miss Daisy: A classic, period-style home with a mix of rich wood trim and wallpaper with detail. Although it's a film set in the 1950s, you can imagine this house working for a family of today—maybe with some new appliances.

Mr. and Mrs. Bridge: Visually rich and captures the elegant yet simple 1950s style the way I imagine that period to be. Merchant Ivory does it again!

The Family Stone: The feeling of a real-life home where family gathers. I have a soft spot for holiday films, but I just like how this house feels real and could very well be where you come home to.

Mr. and Mrs. Smith: A modern take on a couple's style with some urban flair.

Leave Her to Heaven: Terrific use of color, ideal log cabin set on a lake named "Back of the Moon." The whole film has a sort of "watercolor" look to it, and I love that.

Love Actually: Another one I watch every Christmas season. The loft in the film has a great urban look.

The Enchanted Cottage: A magical film about a small cottage. A black-and-white movie, it's an interesting take on the magic of home.

It's Complicated: The main house kitchen and living area make you want to move to California!

Marley and Me: A stone house that is actually a real house, not a set. Great combo of clapboard and stone.

Dan in Real Life: Another great family home setting much like *On Golden Pond*, but with a modern family living in the larger spaces.

Baby Boom: Visually, two distinct examples of styles—the urban locations have one look and color scheme and the Vermont scenes show a whole different style and use of colors.

I love the kitchen in *Something's Gotta Give.*

characters. Watching a film allowed me to travel to far-off places or get a glimpse into what others called home—all from the comfort of my living room. There were certain houses that stuck with me. An early one was Tara, the home in *Gone with the Wind.* This house was made famous by the movie, even though it was just a façade built as a set on the back lot of a Hollywood studio. It touched people, and you felt the power of what home meant for Scarlett O'Hara. I remember looking at that house and thinking, *That's what a house in the Old South must have been like.* The use of color in film was very new when the movie was made in 1939, so the colors seemed a bit more lush and artistic than the black-and-white films I'd been used to. It was like seeing a rich oil painting come to life, and it created a lasting impression. Years later, I was working on a project with an art director, and we went to a movie warehouse where props for movie sets were stored. In the back of a room filled with what seemed like acres of window treatments hung the famous green draperies from the original set of Tara. Seeing them in real life didn't compare to my memory of them. Part of the magic of movies, I suppose.

As I grew older, I realized how films were useful to me creatively to inspire a feeling or theme—the essence of home. Even now, as I prepare a client project or a makeover, I watch a favorite old film as I sketch and work. I'm not looking at the sets for exact details or ideas; rather, they are like old friends—their familiar settings inspire me because they allow me to tap into my imagination. The classic black-and-white films did me a great service because I could use my imagination to decide what the colors on the walls, the furniture, or the scenery might be.

When I speak at events around the country about home and a family-focused lifestyle, I get lots of questions from the audience about how to define their own styles. With all of the home makeover shows on television and magazines that cater to do-it-yourself homeowners, people feel inspired to take on home design, but find themselves blocked by the fundamental issue of knowing their own home style.

I realized that my love of films could be the key to helping homeowners begin to see what they loved. Just as the Look Book can help people determine what they like in a

If you were a set designer or director creating the film setting for your own life story, what would you want your home to look like?

more organized fashion, so films can help them pinpoint ideas for making their homes better. Whenever I watched films, I noticed the settings and the homes. I would watch a movie several times to really appreciate all the layering of details, and many that I watched years ago still remain among my favorites.

If you're stumped by the prospect of defining your personal style, think about films you've seen lately. Did any of them have a house in it that you loved? If so, there was something you were responding to, and it was telling you what you liked.

Just mention the film _Something's Gotta Give_ with Diane Keaton, for example, and people immediately remember the beach house in the film. It had a great look and feel. Although it was a set built in a studio, the house seemed so real that people connected with it in a significant way. The film's director, Nancy Meyers, was often asked about the house during interviews, and it turns out that all the movies she has been associated with have had great houses in them—_Baby Boom_, _Father of the Bride_, and most recently, _It's Complicated_. She obviously has a love of design and the home, but she also goes to great lengths to create settings for the wide variety of characters who live in these homes.

That is a good way to think about your own home design—you and your family are the characters living on your own set. If you were a set designer or director creating the film setting for your own life story, what would you want your home to look like? What would you want the mood to be? How would the setting capture your character and who you are? It's a fun way to think about home design, allowing you to step back and look at your home from a new perspective.

The _Something's Gotta Give_ house captured how many people wanted to see themselves living. They could look at those rooms and be inspired by what they could do in their own spaces no matter what size house they had or where it was located. You may not copy what you see in a movie, but you can notice what you like about it and understand what you are connecting to personally. I suggest watching movies on DVD so you can freeze frames and really study the room images that speak to you.

In that beach-house kitchen set, for example, you might like the white cabinets with the black countertops. You might like the open floor plan that connects the kitchen to the family room and to the views of the outdoors; this gives you an idea for how your spaces could be opened up. You might see how stainless appliances add richness to the space and decide that you'd like to have something similar in your kitchen. You might notice the classic lines of the windows and be inspired to use that type of window in your own renovation. Notice what you respond to as you watch the movie and make a mental note of how you might adapt the ideas.

How might you use a house set as a creative tool? Focus on the interiors instead of the characters and notice the color on the walls, the mix of fabrics, the treatment of floors, the placement of the furniture, even the way the rooms are accessorized with art and props. Once you start picking apart the set and looking at the layers, you start to see how to use those elements in your own way in your own house. Paint color, a furniture grouping, art as a focal point throughout the space—all give you ideas for what you can do at home. Creative visualization for your home empowers you.

The weekend Makeover

When I was a kid I liked moving furniture around. I must have realized even then that change was good. I enjoyed the fact that I could move my bed from one side of the room to the other, use a desk as a bedside table, or bring up a chair from the basement for a new place to read. In every place I have lived since, I have used this approach to keep rooms fresh and interesting. Rearranging the furniture and accessories doesn't cost a thing. You can clean up as you go, and by moving furniture and redistributing accessories, you get an instant new look—and it's a free makeover!

A makeover is something anyone can do instantly. If you want change, then you have to make it happen—now. If you put it off, waiting for a rainy day, weeks and months go by and nothing happens. So you beat yourself up mentally, which bogs you down even more. Time flies . . . so what are you waiting for? Once you do the redesign or makeover, you will definitely ask yourself why you put it off for so long!

Change can be as simple as moving furniture around, or it can be more involved and cost a little more to make the room even better. How much you want to do is up to you. But start in small ways first to build up your designer confidence.

You could have the sofa against the wall, but then move it to the center of the room, stick a console table behind it with a lamp—instant new flow to the space.

If you want change, then you have to make it happen—now.

It could even be as simple as clearing off your coffee table to begin with a clean slate. Then start bringing in props—some art books, bowls of fruit or shells, lanterns with candles, flowers, frames—to create a new focal point. Use what you already have in new ways. Sometimes that's all it takes.

So how do you begin a room makeover? Choose one room that you can tackle over a weekend. You don't want to get overwhelmed by too many projects going on at once. Chaos will not benefit you at this stage. A weekend project gives you an attainable goal.

I am a big believer in documenting your creative projects, so take some digital photos of each phase. Shoot from the same angle each time and choose what you consider the best vantage point for the room.

Here is a sample of how you could break down your makeover. This is something you could do alone, as a fun family project, or with a group of friends. (Instead of a book club, how about forming a makeover club? Meet in a different member's home each month and do a makeover! Just a thought.)

the PLAN
friday night

Grab your Look Book and have it on hand for your creative process.

Make a list of things that are staying in the room (things that you love). Your instincts start kicking in here—you know what you love and do not love. The items you don't love could be stored, sold, donated, etc. If a chair is worn out or doesn't feel right for the room, it's out. However,

that vintage table in the corner is from your vacation in France. You love it, so it stays. Again, follow your instincts about what feels right and wrong.

Important note: Couples or families doing this project together may find that it's a great exercise in learning to be open to the ideas and suggestions of others. It's not personal; it's a chance to be creative and make the space

continues

better for all to enjoy. So if his recliner is on your "out list" and your floral throw pillows are on his, put those things aside in another room for now. Usually, in the end the room looks so good that those things don't need to be brought back in. Remember, it's supposed to be fun, not stressful!

Find the room's focal point (fireplace, windows, built-in with TV, etc.). This will help guide you when you begin putting the room back together. The focal point doesn't have to be based on instincts—it can be what you first see when you walk into the room. In most cases, that's easy to figure out.

Now empty the room of the things that are not coming back. Larger items and accessories can be put in the garage to be moved later to the storage room, basement, or guest room; to be taken to the dump; or to be donated. Or mark the item "free" and put it on the curb. All that should be left are the good things you like for that room. **(1)**

Next, remove the accessories that you like and gather them in one place (such as an adjoining bedroom or dining room). This is your "prop room." The items you put here could include throw pillows, books, art, bedding, lamps, and so on. When they're all in one place, you can start to see things that work well together and perhaps notice a direction for a theme. For example, if you have a few beach-related items, you might want to expand on that as a theme for the room. **(2)**

Now that you have only the larger pieces of furniture in the room, play around with their placement. If you have hardwood floors, put pads or towels under the furniture feet so you can slide pieces without scratching the floor. Use the focal point to guide placement. Create a seating area near the fireplace by moving the sofas around or flanking the fireplace with two chairs. Or, if you have a built-in wall of shelves with the TV as your focal point, arrange the seating with that in mind. Moving pieces around lets you play without making any real commitment. You can see what works where. But it also allows you to see how you might complete an area with pieces you have in other rooms. Say a sofa moved to the center of the room needs a dresser or console table behind it. You realize you have an unused dresser in the garage that could be painted and would be perfect behind the sofa. You might not have enough seating and you realize your guest room has two chairs that might work in this room. Build with what you have on hand. Let go of how the room used to be laid out and open yourself up to seeing it in new ways.

In your search through the house you will also find props and accessories that you could add to your prop room—more books, lamps, frames, and so on—that could make this room complete. This is a good way to involve kids in your makeover. Put them on the search for a certain type of prop. Kids have good instincts about what might be creatively fun, so see what they come up with.

Move the good, larger pieces into a nearby room or put them in the center of the room if need be and cover them up. I find it easier to move things out of the way, but you do whatever works best for you.

It's important to note that if removing an item (a chair, for example) leaves a hole in the new furniture arrangement that you can't fill with a piece from another room, you have a couple of choices. You can save up for the right new piece, have a yard sale and buy a new piece with the proceeds, or just live with an empty spot in the room for a time. That's okay, too. You can always build on the room once you get it started in the right direction.

Now look at the room honestly. Do you need to paint? Do the windows or walls need to be washed? Could the old carpeting be removed to reveal nice floors? What would make that room look better? Do not go overboard by thinking you have to do major construction—it's all about attainable things you can do this weekend.

If you're making over a kitchen, this would be the time to decide whether to paint your cabinets. If so, you would need to apply a primer first and then paint them. Or maybe you paint only the walls for the quick change.

Study your Look Book—are there things that inspire you at this moment that could apply to this room? Maybe a color scheme, a mood, a wall detail, a grouping of frames, a furniture arrangement? You may not do exactly what is on those pages, but you can be inspired visually to re-create it somehow. Again, the Look Book is designed to help you hone in on things you have responded to already. Use it as your creative guide now, helping to keep your instincts in focus.

Look at creative ways to bring in paint. Maybe you could paint one wall a different color and leave the rest alone. You could paint the back of your bookcases a deep color and introduce that hue again on the doors. If you like the color of your walls, you could add a chair rail or plate rail to divide the wall and apply a coordinating shade to the lower part. Paint is one of the fastest, most cost-effective ways to change a room. Do not be afraid of color!

If you are ready for a color change and you like a hue in your throw pillows or your favorite painting, match that color with a paint swatch. Or take the pillow or painting to your local paint store or home improvement store and have paint mixed to match it. If you are not sure about choosing color, find a piece of clothing or an object with a color that you like and use it as your resource.

The goal is to end Friday evening with a clean, empty room so that on Saturday you can paint and or add details as needed. Take a photo of the empty room.

saturday morning

You might be able to get all this done in one day, but if not, you'll have Sunday to finish and to admire your work.

Go to the paint store to get paint and supplies. Not sure what finishes to choose? You can't fail with semigloss for trim and eggshell for walls. If you are an experienced painter, you may not need to tape off window and door frames, baseboards, and crown molding, but do get some tarps to protect the floor. For one room, depending on its size, you may need only one gallon of paint.

If you're adding wood trim, install it before painting. You can add interest to plain walls with inexpensive trim—I've nailed baseboard molding onto plain walls to create a chair rail and vertical strips of lattice to create a raised panel effect.

Painting will go faster if you have one or more helpers. Crank up the music! Have one person start cutting in with a brush while others roll on the paint. You want to move quickly and get this part checked off your list. Depending on the original wall color, you may only need one coat of paint. If not, most paints dry quickly enough that you can apply the second coat a couple of hours after the first.

Take a photo now.

If some of the furniture or props need a new look, prime and paint them now. You could paint and distress that dated hutch or spray-paint those worn-out lamp bases. Take before and after photos of the pieces you transform. **(3)**

continues

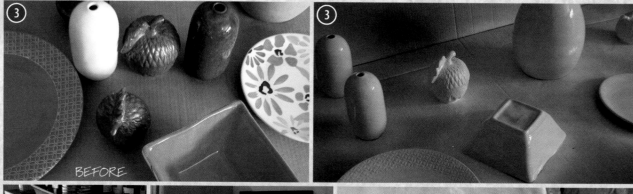

BEFORE

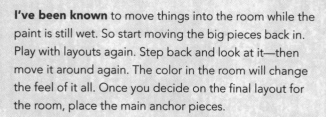

3 BEFORE

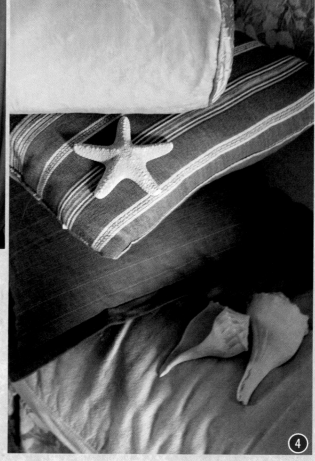

I've been known to move things into the room while the paint is still wet. So start moving the big pieces back in. Play with layouts again. Step back and look at it—then move it around again. The color in the room will change the feel of it all. Once you decide on the final layout for the room, place the main anchor pieces.

Take a photo.

Start bringing in the props and accessories from your prop room. Throw pillows on the sofa, area rugs in certain zones, window treatments if you have them, or lamps on the tables (turn the lamps on now, too). Look at your Look Book images and see how things are styled and laid out. Remember, you want to take a picture of the final room, so think of it the way a magazine or catalog might style it. **(4)**

With the room in this new layout, make a list of the things that you need to get: new window treatments, new lamps, a better area rug, more books, artwork,

mirror, new frames for the family photos to replace the old ones. You may have enough stuff to rework into the room already, but if not, it's okay to spend a little money on this final phase because you can be very creative with a little money. When I'm doing a makeover on the road, I always shop at the same stores and chains. You could spend $100 or $300 and get great results. You do not have to go over the top.

late saturday or on sunday

With your shopping list in hand, go the stores you know will have reasonably priced accessories and props to choose from. Go with a mission. I don't enjoy shopping, but when I'm working on a makeover, I'm on a mission. I want a mirror—I go right to mirrors. I want throw pillows—go there. Don't waste time looking around at things you don't need. Distraction will take away from your makeover.

Follow your instincts here. If you see draperies or a lamp that you instantly like, go for it. When you begin to doubt yourself, walk away! Don't over-think it.

Bring your new stuff into the room. Put up the window treatments, spread out the rugs, hang the artwork (not too high—eye level or lower), add the props, make the bed, whatever is needed. Play around with the placement of things. Try a setup on your coffee table or side table; lay out books on your bookshelves in a creative way; take some new family photos, print them, and frame them. **(5)**

Final touch: Turn on your favorite music, light the candles, light the fire, turn on the lamps, dim the brighter lights. Set the stage. The room is done.

Take the final makeover photo.

You have reached your goal.

Living Room
MAKEOVER

1 Time to put some life into this room. It lacks focus and warmth and feels very temporary.

2 Pull the furniture into the center of the room and add color to the walls. A dark gray blue is sophisticated and contemporary.

3 An area rug anchors the new furniture arrangement near the middle of the room, with the sofa and a new mirror as the focal point. New draperies soften the windows and add a touch of luxury.

4 Over time, a new, smaller-scale chair and ottoman add comfortable, space-saving seating. A console table comes in from elsewhere in the house for a secondary focal point on the end wall. New crystal lamps and silver accessories take the elegance up a notch. Roman shades and sofa pillows add contrasting color and layers of fabric for more warmth.

BEFORE

Dining Room
MAKEOVER

1 With its deep red walls, country French ladder-back chairs, and floral fabric at the windows, this dining room looks dated and tired.

2 The first step in giving the room a facelift is to add beadboard paneling below the chair rail and paint it white to match the existing trim. Sunny yellow paint transforms the upper walls. The hutch is painted white to match.

3 Trim new shades cover the windows for light control and privacy. The country-style ladder-back chairs are replaced with dressier ones inspired by nineteenth-century styles. A distressed-paint finish gives the chairs a cottage look. A round table replaces the old rectangular one to free up more floor space, and a new area rug introduces a touch of blue for a classic yellow, blue, and white scheme. A sleek glass and metal pendant light replaces the old amber-glass chandelier, and new props reinforce the new color scheme.

4 An old bench from the basement gets a new coat of paint and comes into the dining room to serve as a low table.

BEFORE

Family Room
MAKEOVER 1

1 This family room has comfortable seating, good flooring, and nice blinds. But cluttered shelves, unused toys, and a furniture arrangement—detached from any kind of focal point—make the room feel haphazard and unbalanced.

2 Creating a new central seating group anchored by a new area rug and the coffee table puts the focus on gathering and conversation. New drapery panels soften the windows and give the room a more grownup feel. Thinning out the photos and objects on the mantel and bookshelves declutters the room, and a new desk provides additional display space for clean-lined art and books. New lamps distribute light more evenly for a more welcoming effect.

① BEFORE

②

BEFORE

Family Room
MAKEOVER 2

1 Although centered on the television, the seating is poorly placed, including the extra kid-size chairs lined up along one side of the room. The television and table look lost against the blank wall, and the TV table is much too small in scale for the sofa and coffee table. The TV has to stay where it is because of cable and electrical connections, and the table can be used better elsewhere. The coffee table and furniture are keepers, they just need to be better arranged.

2 Bookcases that create the look of a built-in entertainment center give the TV wall a much more appealing look and balance the visual weight of the sofa and coffee table. The new furniture arrangement, anchored by an area rug, gives the room a better focus and shifts the emphasis from the television to conversation. A shelf on the wall behind the sofa displays family photos enlarged to make instant art. The black TV table now serves as a console table behind the sofa. The blue stripe in the sofa provides the key for additional color accents around the room.

3 With a cushion and pillows, the window seat can now actually be used for extra seating. Pulling furniture away from the wall and floating the seating group in the center of the room makes the room feel larger.

Bookcase
MAKEOVER

1 This bookcase is functional but not very engaging visually, and with everything on the same side, the look is lopsided and unbalanced.

2 Stacks of books at varying heights alternate with objects of different sizes and shapes. The objects show off your interests and hobbies and help tell a story about who you are.

Tips for Displays

- Vary the heights of objects to lead the eye along an up-and-down path across the shelf.

- Use objects with different shapes to create variety, but balance the variety with repetition. Here the stacks of books and a painting form rectangular blocks that create stability, while pitchers and a model sailboat introduce curving lines.

- To create depth and movement, set some objects further back into the bookshelf than others. That leads the eye forward and backward, which makes for a more intriguing display.

- Use repeating colors to unify a display. Here the white pitchers and white book spines provide overall unity.

- Cover old books with parchment paper (like the old days of covering your school books with brown paper). This gives the whole book display a stylish, unified look.

- Arrange items to lead the eye from one shelf to another as well as across each shelf. Here the repeating stacks of books take your eye from top to bottom and back again.

- Instead of using a single large object, you can cluster a few smaller ones and achieve a similar visual weight. Use odd numbers of objects for the most interesting results.

- Arrange items to lead the eye from one shelf to another as well as across each shelf. Here the repeating stacks of books take your eye from top to bottom and back again.

- Try leaning art work or photographs against the back of the bookcase or against a stack of books. Or alternate a shelf of books with a shelf of art in simple frames propped against the back of the bookcase.

- Paint the background of your bookcases a new color to make a dramatic statement in the room. For example, if you love a red wall, but do not want to paint the whole room that color—bookcases or other built-ins with backgrounds can get the special treatment instead.

① BEFORE

②

CREATIVE
thoughts

Some fun, instant-makeover things to think about . . .

1 Take a boring white-walled room and add some simple molding to the walls. Use this trim piece as a divider between two tones of paint. It's easy and really adds visual interest to the room.

2 Instant sofa makeover: If you have a sofa with removable back pillows, try replacing them with various sizes of throw pillows, both large and small, and create a grouping at the back of your sofa. This gives you a new look, new color and texture, and saves having to buy a new sofa.

3 Props don't have to be fancy or expensive. A soup bowl or platter filled with river rocks makes a great focal point.

4 Outdoor furniture can be used inside in creative ways. If you don't have the money to buy all new furniture for a room, look at your patio furniture. Clean it up, paint it, add new cushions, and give your room a new look.

5 De-clutter—this is an instant makeover in itself. Simplify areas where you have too much "stuff" going on and see what a difference it makes (not pictured).

6 Mix and match furniture—wicker, wood, fabric-covered, metal. Contrasting textures keep things interesting.

7 If you have built-ins or cabinets with drawer pulls or knobs, replace them with new ones for an instant new look. All you need is a screwdriver. Take the old hardware with you when you shop so you can make sure the new hardware will fit the old holes (not pictured).

8 You can give a sink a whole new look with a new faucet. It's a great way to modernize a kitchen quickly and inexpensively.

9 Bring color into your room easily with throw pillows or window treatments.

chapter 4

Redesign or Renovate?

aking change happen in your home is good, but when you are in the midst of renovating or redesigning your home, you may not feel that it is such a good thing. Big change can be stressful. Your house may be turned upside down, with dust covering everything, all your possessions in boxes, and contractors walking in and out.

I can fully understand why people get stressed out over renovations or even simple redesigns, because there is a certain amount of upheaval involved. Having to make choices on products and projects adds to the stress. The basic routine of your household is interrupted, too. The truth is that change is scary for some people, which is why many homes stay exactly the same year after year, even though the homeowner might want to make changes.

The more you know about what you want to do, the more empowered you will feel—and feeling empowered can help reduce stress.

What if you could know that change would do you good and that it doesn't have to be as stressful as you think? From my experience on many design projects, I've learned that feeling empowered can help reduce stress—and what makes you feel empowered are preparation and information. The more you know about what you want to do, the more empowered you will feel. That confidence can benefit you whether you have a designer's eye or no creative ability whatsoever. The process isn't perfect and will have its moments of tension, but certainly you can live through it if you know as much as you can going into it and stay focused during the turnaround.

The first thing to decide is how big a renovation you want to do. You might want an addition on the back of your house or you might just want to redesign one room or area. Obviously the size of the project determines how much money you'll need to spend.

*How big a renovation do you want to do?

*A renovation in progress

Focus in on the area that will be changed. What is the first priority? You might long to have a larger kitchen or master bedroom, but does that need to happen now or should other things fall into line first, such as upgrading the flooring and windows in other rooms? What makes the most sense now?

At the same time, think about how the changes can affect the value of your house if you were to sell it. You may find that on your street, putting a major addition on your house would make it too expensive for your neighborhood. You don't want to spend a lot on a renovation and have no chance of recouping your investment. However, if the upgrades or changes are more cosmetic, then you could be adding value to the house by improving what a potential buyer is looking for. Updates or improvements to kitchens, bathrooms, moldings, flooring, and heating systems can all enhance the resale value of the house.

For those shopping for a new home, if you're not finding exactly what suits you, could an addition or renovation make a house you *kind of like* into a house you can fall in love with? If the price is perfect but the house has limitations, try seeing it in new ways—look for its potential. Maybe walls can come down between rooms to open up spaces, simple changes can update bathrooms, or wall-to-wall carpet can get pulled up to reveal wood floors. If the price of the house is low enough, even costly renovations such as installing new windows or doors, updating electrical and plumbing systems, or adding square footage to make a smaller house more functional may be worth the investment in the long run.

As you plan your redesign, think long range. Sometimes a renovation can be *phase 1* of a larger-scale remodel that takes place over time as you have the money. You might have a great backyard but your living room doesn't have windows that show it off well, so installing a series of French doors and windows would transform it nicely in phase 1. Later on, you might add a screened porch outside the French doors where you have a deck now—phase 2. Phase 3 could include new landscaping or a pool.

Once you have decided to renovate and you know which area you want to focus on, decide how much you can afford to spend. Is the project big enough that you need to refinance your mortgage or take out a loan? Do you have a chunk of money saved for this renovation? It's not worth overextending yourself money-wise if the debt is going to keep you from enjoying the result comfortably. One way to cut down on costs is to do some of the work yourself. As you refine your plans, decide which parts of the project you have the skills and time to do yourself and which parts are best hired out.

Once you have determined what you want to do and how much money you have to spend on it, it's time to review your Look Book (refer to Chapter 2) or start a vision board with images or ideas that you're dreaming about for a room. You want to get a visual sense of what you are trying to achieve. Keep in mind that the images do not have to be exactly like what you want to create. If you're designing a family room and your inspiration room is much larger than what you have to work with, look at the colors used, the window styles, the furniture layout, how built-ins are used, moldings, and so on to guide you as you begin your "goal list" for your project. This is part of empowering yourself with information about what you want.

The goal list will help you see what your priorities are. I'm a big fan of making lists of things I need to get done. When I complete something, I highlight it instead of crossing it off so I can see that tasks have been finished.

Planning a Big Renovation

Here are some things to consider.

- Draw up rough plans. Have a basic plan in place to be able to communicate to contractors and others about what you are trying to do. You can draw up rough plans yourself or ask a friend to help out.

- Find a general contractor. Get a few estimates for the job. Referrals from friends or family are a great place to start the search. Also, if you have seen a renovation in your town, stop and ask the homeowners who they worked with and whether it was a good experience. You want to find a contractor you connect with because you need to be able to communicate with this person for a long period and during moments of making big decisions. Sometimes relying on your first impression is

helpful—at least until the contractor sends you his or her estimate. (Alternatively, you can break down the project and act as your own general contractor, but that takes extra coordination, getting everyone in for estimates and keeping them on track as the project gets going.) Once you have a few people lined up, set up a time to talk about the project. Be clear about what you want and try to remain focused. Then ask for a detailed estimate in writing of what the contractor will do for you.

- Line up subcontractors. Sometimes a general contractor will have teams that he works with regularly for electrical, plumbing, drywall, painting, and so on. Or the general contractor might want you to handle hiring the subcontractors. It will vary. Certainly it makes it easier if a contractor has a team or contacts who are used to working with him to keep things running smoothly. If your contractor has contacts, ask whether he will include their estimates in his quote; if so, you would pay him, and he would then pay the subcontractors. If you deal with the subcontractors, get their estimates in writing and get references. Always check references; you don't want to hire someone who doesn't show up for work or who doesn't do good work.

- Determine whether you need architectural renderings. If you are adding on to the existing footprint of your house, architectural drawings may be required by code in order to get a building permit. A local builder can tell you what your city or town requires. If you do need drawings, ask friends and family for referrals. Sometimes architects will give you a quote for coming up with a set of drawings that reflect your ideas (without their creative input). For a complicated remodel, however, you may want someone who can be more involved and contribute ideas. Just know that you'll have to pay for that extra service and attention.

- Find out what permits you need from your town. If you are building new construction or doing electrical and plumbing work, the town will send inspectors to sign off on various phases during your renovation. You can get the permits and deal with inspectors yourself, or your contractor may include that in the services he or she provides.

- If you are doing a kitchen or bathroom that requires cabinets and other built-in pieces, consult a kitchen designer or showroom for help with layouts and ordering the right products. This is another way of lowering your stress level. Kitchen designers are experts at planning these spaces, and they may have great advice or solutions you might not have thought of.

- If you are building a room or installing windows, flooring, doors, and so on, research what's available locally and online. If you are looking for a certain type of window, for example, take your Look Book to your local lumberyard or home improvement store and see what they carry. Or search online to see who might sell what you aspire to have.

- Think about timing. How much time will this project take? Is it the right season for construction where you live? Some builders are busy in summer but less so in winter and may give you a better quote. Some people want to have their renovation done in time for Thanksgiving or Christmas. Will you need to move out for a time? Stay with friends during big construction? Is there a time that might be less invasive for your family routine? For example, summer months might mean everyone is home, so construction would interfere with vacation plans. In the fall, the kids will be in school. A renovation can mean that extra people will be in your house for many weeks. Some people get stressed having people underfoot, so think about what might work better for you and what you can honestly cope with.

Start a Shopping List

Now think about products and items that you may need and start a general list. For example:

- Insulation. If you are adding on or gutting a room you'll probably have to insulate it. Look at options to meet your needs.

- Drywall or plaster walls. If you have an older home that already has plaster walls, you may want to continue that. Sometimes the choice is based on where you live: In some parts of the country, drywall is more common; in others, it's plaster. It is worth asking your builder for a quote on both. Sometimes builders can install the drywall themselves, but will subcontract plaster to another team. Don't be afraid to ask. There are no ignorant questions. It is your home and your money.

- Doors and windows. What kind of exterior doors might you need? Do you want standard solid doors, French doors, or sliding doors? Where would new windows go? What style do you want (casement, double-hung, awning style, sliders)? What about interior doors? If you opt for solid wood doors, you still have a choice between slab or raised panels. Can you

*Add country character with beadboard wainscoting and a chair rail

save space with pocket doors? How might glass doors or recycled vintage doors enhance the look of your space? This is why I think even doing a rough sketch helps you remember what you are considering. Get it out of your head and onto paper. Usually the contractor will prep and install doors and windows for you as part of the project.

- Lighting and electronics. Do you have any special needs for lighting, new dimmer switches, sound systems or a plasma TV? Can you simply update fixtures or will you need to relocate lighting, which will affect the budget? Although you won't have to pick out fixtures at the start, it does help to have a sense of where you will want lighting to go, as well as switches and outlets.

- Flooring. What kind of flooring will you choose— hardwood, laminate, vinyl, stone, tile, or carpet? There are many options to choose from and many levels of cost. It is really all about what is right for you and your budget. Do you want an earth-friendly product, or have you seen a surface material that you must have in your new space? Gather up ideas of what you love. Search online for options and information, but buy locally if possible to save money on shipping and to avoid having to wait for special orders to come in. Some companies will install their product themselves. They send a representative to measure your space and give you an estimate. When the product is ready for installation, they send a team to put it in quickly.

- Details. Do you want a certain type of molding or trim? Trim and moldings can add visual value to any room, but this can add to your budget because of materials used and labor for the builder to cut and install the trimwork properly. Think about whether you just need moldings to finish off around windows and doors, or if you want to introduce nice crown molding and a more pronounced baseboard. Most windows and doors need some sort of trim to finish off the edges. You can do a basic ranch-style molding that is pretty simple, or you can upgrade to a fancier or more elaborate profile. Visit your local home improvement store and see what appeals to you. Are you thinking about other architectural details, such as raised-panel walls, beadboard, or chair rails? Do you need built-ins such as a bookcase, entertainment center, or window seat that can be finished off with trim and detailing? These are things a builder would construct or install for you, but be sure to include them for the estimate. They will make your estimate more costly, but can add to your enjoyment of the space as well as to the resale value of your home.

Start a vision board. The more organized you are at the start, the less scattered you will feel.

- Cabinets. If you are redoing a kitchen or bathroom, look at options you like in your Look Book and online. Visit local showrooms and see what is available. Cabinets can be purchased as stock items or as custom or semi-custom items. Custom cabinets are the most expensive and will take the most time for delivery. This is where kitchen designers might come in handy. Look at photos of kitchens they have designed and, if possible, visit some in person. Bring your Look Book to your meeting.

- Appliances. If you are renovating your kitchen, you will have to know the look you want and what appliances you need—dishwasher, wine cooler, beverage refrigerator, microwave, wall oven, warming drawers? Do you want an electric or gas range? How many burners or ovens do you need? Does the fridge need to be side by side with the freezer, or do you want the fridge on top with a freezer drawer at the bottom? Do you want stainless, black, white (or other colors)? Do you want the refrigerator door to match the cabinetry?

- Countertops. Your Look Book can help you focus on colors and perhaps even materials, but also look at countertop options in person to see whether you like the appearance and feel of various materials. If you are planning the space with a kitchen designer, he or she can show you the options and discuss the pros and cons of each. Also consider how much cleaning and maintenance you want to do. For example, tile is easy to clean and heat-resistant, but it's hard to keep the grout clean. Butcher block adds warmth to a space, but it gets scratched and needs to be oiled. Granite is elegant looking and is heat and scratch resistant, but needs to be sealed periodically. Concrete counters offer a wide variety of finishes and colors, but they require expert installation, can be as expensive as granite, and show wear and stains.

- Paint. Start thinking about paint colors. White trim with colored walls? Tone on tone for trim and walls? Paint the ceiling white or bring in some color there? Painted floors in some areas? Specialty paint effects? Faux finishes? Assemble a palette you are leaning toward. Painting is one of the last parts of a renovation job, and if you want to save money, plan on doing it yourself.

You could get the builder to give you the price of priming the walls and plan on doing the final color yourself. However, if you can get a great price for painting—treat yourself and save your energy! Many homes have white trim and molding to contrast with the wall color. What about painting the trim and molding a lighter shade in the same color family as the wall? However, if you have new windows and doors for your renovation, they may come with a white finish already applied—so keep the trim white to match the windows and doors.

- Furniture. You can start thinking about how you might furnish the room, but keep it broad to start with—you may find that details or needs for furniture change as the project proceeds.

Renovation Projects

Here are a few renovation projects that show some of the directions you can go in: tearing out walls and adding on, turning an unused space into a functional room, taking charge of your own design and renovation, or showing how simple changes in a quick cosmetic redesign can make a big impact.

The Big Renovation—Adding On

This renovation project started with the kitchen, a small, cramped space dating to the 1960s. After making improvements elsewhere in the house, the family finally decided it was time to deal with the kitchen. The question was, should they do more than just re-do the kitchen? Finally, they decided that if they were going to stay there, they should make it the place of their dreams. (See Chapter 6, "Everyday Kitchens," and Chapter 7, "Dining In," for more views.) They opted for building an addition that would add 10 feet to the back of the whole house. This would open up the kitchen footprint and expand their present living room and dining areas, plus give them room for a full guest bathroom and a larger room for their child.

The contractor they chose gave them an estimate for the addition priced by the foot (a certain dollar amount per square foot of the addition). Each contractor will estimate differently, however, and it is very important to get everything in writing, from demolition to framing, finishing, plumbing, electrical, and painting costs. A detailed estimate will help you decide where you can cut costs if necessary by eliminating some items or making substitutions. For example, you may want high-end appliances but you can only afford a less expensive line; or instead of the hardwood floors you wanted, you install carpet and plan for hardwood floors later. You can also save money by doing some of the work yourself, such as demolition, taking down drywall, or installing trim.

After several months of living in the midst of construction, this family had a finished space that completely changed the feel of their home. It also added to the value of their house should they ever sell it, but more importantly, it made the house their dream home.

*A creative seating option—a built-in banquette

BEFORE

It is very important to get everything in writing, from demolition to framing, finishing, plumbing, electrical, and painting costs.

*The 10 foot addition across the back of the house allowed for a new open floor plan

Use What You Have: Attic Space

For this renovation, the focus was on making an unused attic space functional. This bonus space was used for storing extra furniture, clothes, and Christmas decorations, but because it was uninsulated, it was cold during the winter. Also, it had no windows with views.

The homeowners wanted a home office and had thought about building a small barn on their property for that purpose. They had even considered converting their garage into a home office. But one day they began looking at the attic and realized that if they cleared it out completely, they might have something to work with. With the boxes and furniture removed, they could see the footprint of what could be created there—a home office with a view. Removing an old cedar closet revealed the brick wall of the chimney. They decided to keep the brick exposed to add warmth and a rustic feel to the remodeled space.

The vision for the raw open space included an open work area for desks, seating, a drafting table, and a work island, as well as a storage room and a sleeping nook in the corner. The homeowners had to decide whether to divide the space with walls or keep it open and loftlike. Drawings of various layouts helped them settle on keeping the space open but creating zones to make the room more intimate. They also decided to give the new area a Southwestern look.

*Adding a dormer

*Hidden brick chimney

*Windows needed to let in light

*Knee walls needed

BEFORE

*Exposed brick chimney
adds a rustic feel

*New windows
with a classic look

*Knee walls
allow for
furniture
placement

*Room divided into zones for
working and relaxing

*Central island for working

The first phase involved framing the room. Walls and knee walls had to be built to allow for furniture placement, and the staircase and storage room needed to be sectioned off from the main office area. Adding a dormer for four new windows and a drafting table required cutting a large hole in the roof to make way for new construction. Once that was done, natural light poured into the room and revealed views of the surrounding countryside. To let in even more light, the two air vents on each side of the brick chimney were turned into windows, and a new set of windows for the sleeping nook was installed where an old attic vent fan had been.

Working with their existing lighting sources, the homeowners first decided where they wanted to put their computers and office equipment. Then they figured out their lighting plan by determining what kind of lighting they needed for the various work surfaces and seating areas. You can work with your electrician to figure out a design plan that makes sense for your needs and layout. Remember, a well-thought-out lighting plan is important in setting any room's mood and is something you will appreciate when the room is completed.

Looking at their space from a new perspective empowered the homeowners to make better use of what they already had. It also gave them a functional, well-designed office just steps away from their living space. The following images highlight some of the decisions they made during the renovation process.

*Insulation was installed to keep the room warm in winter and cool in summer

*Cleaned up old brick chimney

*New knee walls

*Mudding the drywall sealed gaps and seams, and then the walls were primed.

*Although painting was an option, the homeowners chose to apply a clay product that would reinforce the Southwestern theme and make an eco-friendly wall finish.

*An all-natural, environmentally friendly product was tinted to the homeowners' specifications and applied to the walls in a two-day process

*As the furniture was placed and the room styled, the attic began to feel as if it had always been that way.

*The walls have a rich texture that changes with the light.

*New lighting installed

*Salvaged barn wood for window trim

*After the walls dried, wood flooring was installed.

*A pair of vents that flanked the brick chimney were replaced with windows that now welcome natural light into attic

Do It for Yourself: Kitchen Remodel

This kitchen shows what you can accomplish when you take charge of a renovation and follow your instincts about what you want and like. For an overview of the space, see top photo on page 38. The house was probably built in the 1980s, with the kitchen and the rooms around it separated by walls. Because the homeowners love to cook and entertain, they knew they wanted to open up the rooms to make one large space with the kitchen at the center. They also love nature, and their home is surrounded by woodlands, so they wanted to use a tree trunk as part of the structure of the space. Remodeling became a dance between defining their ideas and goals and finding a builder-contractor who was willing to try creative ways of doing things.

In the newly opened space, the homeowners created a central kitchen that was open on all sides. On one side they placed bar seating adjacent to the family room; on another, the cooking range opens to the casual dining area, with a view to the outside. On a third side, the kitchen opens to the foyer and living room beyond. A storage cabinet divides the kitchen from the foyer and provides the perfect place to mount a large-screen TV. The remaining wall accommodates cabinets, an appliance garage, and the refrigerator. For these homeowners, the goal of renovation was all about the overall experience of entering the heart of the home and feeling welcomed into an exciting, creative space.

*Storage below the cooktop emphasizes the beauty and creative use of wood

*Custom-designed concrete countertops feature crushed blue glass for sparkle and color

*Countertops at different levels suit different tasks

*Track-system lighting recalls the set of a TV cooking show

*A real tree trunk on a stone base serves as a load-bearing column

*Spotlights and pendants provide dramatic lighting

*Staves from old wine barrels were recycled to build the corner feature

*A tree root forms the table base

A real tree trunk rests on a rock (literally, a rock) and serves as both a physical and creative support for the open kitchen plan. It also adds uniqueness to the space because it is unexpected. Another fun twist on the typical kitchen is the use of a track system for the main lighting over the work area. The grid with lights and wires attached to it (including the speakers for the music) creates the feeling of a set for a TV cooking show. The studio feel captures the fun atmosphere the homeowner/musician was striving for. Best of all, everything is on dimmers!

Layers of light bring the room to life, magically creating a mood for each area. At every turn, the details reveal the family's willingness to try new ideas and unusual approaches: beautiful wood grain in the cabinet construction and design, open storage cubbies suspended by sailboat cable wire on the dining room wall, a glass dining table with a base made from a tree root—not to mention the incorporation of the tree as a support column. The panel of wood planks in the dining area was made from old wine barrels from Napa—another illustration of taking what could be a boring, unused wall area and making it a visual detail that adds character to the room. It also warms the space with another layer of wood tones.

The concrete countertops are another detail with a story. The homeowners made them themselves, along with their builder, choosing the tint and texture they wanted and even going so far as to crush cobalt blue glass water bottles to add to the concrete. The result gives off an unexpected sparkle of blue along the countertops. Details like these, with great stories behind them, become part of the journey of renovation and make the results unique.

*Cubbies supported with cable wire (used on sailboats) provide unusual open storage with a great look

This is a great example of a project where the homeowners follow their creative instincts and go for it!

Easy Fix: Kitchen Facelift

This space needed a facelift, but the homeowners didn't want to spend a lot of money on major construction. They began by looking at what was good about the space and what could be made better. The appliances didn't need to be replaced; they were fairly new and basic white. The wood floors just needed buffing. The countertops were also in good shape and added richness to the room. The cabinets had already been painted white, and new hardware would easily perk them up. One obvious, easy improvement was to paint the dark green walls a warm, golden yellow that makes the room feel sunnier.

New lighting also helps make this room feel larger and fresher. Simply changing the overhead light in the center of the room to halogen spotlights focuses attention on the island area, cabinets, and cooking utensils. Changing out the fixture over the sink to a hanging schoolhouse pendant adds visual interest. A layer of under-cabinet lighting banishes shadows from corners and illuminates food-prep surfaces. Two other quick changes make a big difference to the look: Store-bought shelving and brackets turn a previously blank wall into a new open display area for everyday dishware and glassware, and changing an old sink faucet to a more modern one updates the sink area.

The changes in this kitchen space show what can be done in a week or even a weekend. It's a good example of how simple changes can dramatically give a space a new lease on life.

*Shelving adds display space to a blank wall

BEFORE

*The dark green walls were painted a golden yellow to brighten the kitchen

*New lighting focuses attention on the island area

*Bare windows show off classic lines and let light in

*New hardware on drawers and cabinets gives a new look instantly

COOKIES

BREAD

Part II
Rooms of the House

chapter 5

Living Family Rooms

I think that living rooms and family rooms are right up there with kitchens for being the heart of any home. Families spend a great deal of time in these spaces. In the old days, however, the living room was only used on special occasions. It was off limits to kids and was not always the most inviting room of the house, with its stiff furniture and fragile accessories. The older homes in the neighborhood where I grew up had two living rooms, or parlors, one in the front and one in the back. They opened to each other, but one was more formal and one was where the radio and eventually the television were. I remember being a kid and going to these houses at Christmas. The tree would be in the front room, which was hardly used the rest of the year, and the guests would be in the other room.

At our house, I remember the living room being the epitome of the trends of the 1970s. Yet I could walk across the street to Mrs. Blanchard's house and see design that was unchanged since the 1940s, classic and All-American in style. Obviously, this all had some sort of influence on me and helped me to know more about what I liked and didn't like.

At first we didn't have a family room, but eventually my dad finished our basement as a family room, with wood paneling and a Franklin stove. I loved it because I felt that I was going to some rustic lodge in the mountains. As I write this in my own home years later, with the fire going in the fireplace, I remember sitting in that paneled room by the Franklin stove and reading old textbooks about remodeling and home repairs and doing my floor-plan sketches. Everything comes full circle, I suppose. In any event, that room said to me that I was home.

When family rooms were no longer enough for the more casual lifestyle of the modern era, the great room came along. This room seemed to never end, flowing from wall to wall to make one big room that included the kitchen, the dining room, a breakfast area, and the family room all in one. Certainly it gave the idea of more space, but it also created many problems in terms of design and layout. How do you paint that kind of room? Where do you end one color and begin another when there is no clear stopping point between spaces? How do you furnish it to make it inviting? The safe haven. The gathering space. That is what living family rooms are.

The safe haven. The gathering space. That is what living family rooms are.

Now what I'm seeing are rooms that mean something. The spaces are not as vast and uninviting as they've been in the recent past. People are definitely leaning more toward intimate areas that are warm and inviting, easy on the eye and the mood (not to mention on design style). Individual rooms lend themselves to different design themes if that's what you want, but creating rooms with specific functions that serve the way you live is really what good home design is all about today.

Design for living rooms or family rooms isn't about a certain style or a certain look, it's about *living rooms* that live and breathe, that are a part of a real family's life, and *family rooms* that connect families.

The rooms in this chapter capture the essence of how families live today, no matter how big or small their houses are. I love the fact that people are making these spaces their own. It's like I always say, you can't control the outside world, but you can create a world on the inside that is good to you and your family. The safe haven. The gathering space. That is what living family rooms are.

Zoned for Living

Even though the latest trend is toward individual rooms and intimate spaces, there are still many, many homes with great rooms or family rooms—one big space with areas that serve a certain purpose—maybe a kitchen, a living area, and an eating area. It's great to look at, but for everyday living this large space can be a nightmare because it's a huge blank canvas.

So where do you begin? In the home on these pages, the space divided naturally into three distinct areas: the kitchen, the dining area, and the main living-family room. The open flow makes this a wonderful house for entertaining, and dividing it into these zones keeps it from feeling too cold and vast for everyday living.

The kitchen, of course, defines itself, and once the table and chairs are in place, the dining area is established. That leaves the main living area as a large stage to fill. To do this successfully, think about how you move through the space. In this house, the natural flow from the entrance to the kitchen is a direct line. To leave this path clear, I divided the main living area into a larger seating area to the right and a smaller one to the left and anchored each with a large area rug. This left the wood floor in between as an open walkway to the kitchen and the dining area.

When you're considering how to deal with a large, open space, stand at the entrance and notice any focal points that draw your eye. It may be a fireplace, a piece of furniture, a seating area, or a window with a great view. Here, I wanted to create layers or "moments" that would stop the eye and not immediately give away the fact that the dining room was toward the back. An inviting seating area in the middle of the room does that. It acts as a focal point as well as a visual divider, a buffer for the dining area beyond.

The sofa also allows for a console table and additional seating behind it to create layers and visual interest. From this point, furnishing the room is a matter of building out from the sofa. An oversized storage ottoman doubles as a coffee table in front of the sofa, and unmatched side chairs round out the seating group. A large cabinet with table lamps goes in front of the windows to add warmth against the backdrop of large windows. In some homes the fireplace would be the obvious focal point, but in this case, because it was right by the front door, I decided to lead the eye to the main seating area first. The fireplace becomes a secondary focal point when guests are seated on the sofa. The final touches—pillows, books, art, accessories—are the props that make you feel at home.

To take this room to next level, the owners could easily paint the walls a darker tone throughout and add window treatments. Of course, changing out seasonal decorations keeps the mood of the room fresh, too.

When you're considering how to deal with a large, open space, stand at the entrance and notice any focal points that draw your eye.

*The large rug anchors this seating area

*This ottoman doubles as a coffee table

The fun part about a room like this one is that you can move furniture around to create new zones and give the space a whole new feeling. The small seating area to the left of the main one is a perfect casual gathering spot, but the dining table could go here instead. Or this spot could be reconfigured to accommodate an armoire with a TV, a couple of chairs, and ottomans. I am always changing furniture around in my own house. It keeps things new, and it's a chance to be creative. Plus, it's a great workout!

Lighting a vast area is a key consideration. In this room there are overhead lights on dimmers. These provide a good overall light as a background, but it's also important to light the individual zones. The kitchen has under-cabinet lights to illuminate countertops. In the dining area, candlelight and decorative lamps on a side table provide mood lighting. In the main seating area, lamps on the console table behind the sofa provide light for reading, games, and conversation. By the fireplace, a floor lamp or a smaller lamp on a side table provides reading light. The candlestick lamps on the cabinet in front of the windows create a cozy glow at night and help balance the light around the space so it feels evenly illuminated.

IDEAS
you can look for and use

Notice how the fabrics in the furniture are mixed? You can have a basic, neutral tone on the sofa and add rich textures on throw pillows. Try partnering chairs in solid fabrics with some upholstered in a pattern or in leather. Bring wooden chairs into the mix, too, for richness and variety.

You don't have to cover up all your windows, especially if you have great views. Install shades that pull up out of the way by day yet add privacy at night.

Overstuffed furniture or larger-scale furniture serves you well in large spaces like this one. It's okay to mix in smaller pieces, but a few large pieces will anchor the space.

Rugs also anchor an area. I love sisal rugs, but in this case the room needed the added dimension of color from area rugs. Do your rugs take over the room, or could adding them bring it together?

Does a room like this need to be all one color? No, but I could certainly see a darker sand color on all the walls. I think having a consistent wall color allows the pieces in the room to speak for themselves.

——— Room for Living and Playing ———

When I walked into this family's home, I was very impressed with how inviting it felt. The house is a classic suburban house, but the furnishings gave it a surprisingly modern look.

This family's living room is very much a room that they live in and play in. With young kids and a dog, the family needs a space that is easy to maintain for everyday family living, yet stylish and up-to-date for the grownups, too. So how do they achieve that happy balance given a hectic family life?

An eating area/crafting area defines one zone. A seating area with a fireplace defines another for watching TV and playing with toys. Neutral colors and fabrics make for a calming color scheme. Uncluttered spaces and clean-lined, simple details give the room an organized feeling.

The family can gather to play games, share a snack, or do an art project, yet the backdrop is well thought out and inviting, with family photos in the fireplace built-ins and a comfortable seating area for snuggling in and watching *Finding Nemo* on a rainy day. Grownup space, yet kid-friendly at the same time.

Furniture placement is key for a room that functions well. Choosing the right pieces of furniture is also important. A sectional sofa may not be right for every room, but it works well here because it allows seating to focus on the TV and the fireplace at the same time. Focal points help organize a room. In this room the fireplace is the focal point and the room is built around that.

*Dining table doubles as craft area

*Sectional sofa anchors seating area

IDEAS
you can look for and use

With a neutral palette of color on the furniture, you can bring in color with throw pillows, throws, picture frames, artwork, area rugs, lampshades, and so on. When you get tired of that scheme, you can change it easily without buying all new furniture.

Do you need to change your window treatments? I'm a big fan of 2–inch-wide white wooden blinds. Their classic look goes with various styles.

Do you have nicely framed photos or kids' art on your walls? This is a cost-effective way to bring personal style into your family room. Get nice frames with white mats to make the art or photo stand out.

Put your feet up. Do you have washable fabrics on your furniture? If you have kids or pets, upholstery will need to be cleaned. That's why I recommend slipcovered sofas and chairs. You can pop the slipcovers into the wash, and they get better with each washing.

Do you have enough storage for all those DVDs, CDs, toys, and books? Ottomans make great hidden storage, built-ins are perfect, and TV cabinets with baskets or drawers are a good solution, too.

Do you have a crafting or art closet near your family room? Create an area for art supplies and games. Keep them close by to inspire kids and adults to be creative. Have a family night that is all about doing an art project together.

Music in the family room—turn it up and enjoy some music time together.

Inspire and motivate your kids to read by keeping baskets of children's books handy.

Mountain Lodge

This home (also shown in the top photo on page 58) is a great example of design reflecting its environment, but it's also a source of ideas for creating a design that transports you to another place. It's the kind of house you want to escape to after a snowstorm or a day of skiing. If you love that look or mood, here are the keys to creating it, even if you're miles from snow or ski slopes.

Starting with a theme can make it easier for your inner designer to come out and be creative.

- A massive, two-story flagstone fireplace with a weathered timber for the mantel defines the room's rugged character and alludes to mountain country outside.
- Salvaged barn-board floors, stripped, sanded, and stained, give the room vibrancy and warmth. Wide planks visually expand the space and suggest a Colonial-era home, when century-old timber yielded wider boards.

- Rough, dark-stained beams and exposed rafters recall the structure of old barns. Using salvaged wood brings instant history to a new home.
- Lots of windows welcome light and showcase great views.
- Creamy walls and built-ins balance the rustic elements and emphasize the open, airy feeling. A cathedral ceiling enhances the expansive quality.
- Add props and visual cues in artwork, sleds, old skis, and so on that convey the theme you are striving for.

Another thing I like about this home is the love for animals that is evident everywhere (especially by the fireplace, where the dogs get the best seats). Being a dog lover myself, I am always intrigued by how people integrate their pets into their worlds. My dog makes himself at home every night on the sofa, which is why I have fabrics and coverings that are washable. When you're making choices about surfaces and furnishings, think about how your pets live in your space. Hardwood floors, for example, are beautiful and allow you to keep things clean, but they can get scratched up by big dogs running around.

Carpeting isn't a perfect solution, either—it can get stained and certainly look pretty lived-in with pets around. Do you need to keep your dogs contained in one part of the house? I once saw a mudroom that had a Dutch door separating the mudroom from the rest of the house. The lower half stayed closed to keep kids out and dogs in, yet the top could remain open.

This living room also offers a great lesson in the possibilities of furniture arrangement. Imagine it without all the furniture, and you'll see the good bones—the hardwood floors, the soaring windows, the massive stone fireplace. This is the kind of space I could see rearranging seasonally, depending on traffic flow. In summer the doors to the outside need to be easily accessible, but in winter they might not be used as much or at all. The way the room is now puts the focus on the fireplace and visually separates the living area from the eating area. In summer, move the sofa opposite the French doors, and you open the room to the outdoors and the view. An area rug could be brought in to change the color scheme a bit or anchor the seating group more firmly in front of the fireplace.

Starting with a theme, such as a mountain lodge or beach house, can make it easier for your inner designer to come out and be creative. If a theme allows you to see clearly what you want to create, you are on the right track. You might begin with a piece of artwork that inspires you, a piece of fabric with colors and details that set your creative wheels in motion, or even a piece of furniture.

This room makes me imagine sitting by the fire with chocolate chip cookies and milk while a snowstorm howls outside. When you sit in your family room, where are you transported to?

IDEAS
you can look for and use

Architectural salvage is a great way to add character to new construction. Staircases, windows, cabinets, flooring, lighting, mantels, and trim add a sense of history. Even simple touches, such as a weathered beam for a mantel, can add a layer of interest to a room.

If you are building a home with a new fireplace, think about the kind of finish you want. This one is local fieldstone. A more economical choice would be to cover the chimney breast with drywall and put your money into a fancy wood mantel.

If you are redoing an old, outdated-looking fireplace, consider using faux stone veneers (think of veneers as just the face of the stones). They come in many styles and colors—try a few samples to see what style is right for your space and theme. The result can look just as real as heavy fieldstones. I once installed stone veneer over an old brick fireplace and loved the result. It was like putting a puzzle together with stones. In the end, it looked like it had always been there.

Notice the rich red accent colors in this room. If you love a color but feel that it would be too much to have it on the walls or furniture, bring it in with accessories.

Pets need a place, too. Dog beds and areas for the dogs to curl up are fun and create a relaxed atmosphere.

Built-ins are great for displaying accessories and also for helping blend technology such as TVs and stereos into the wall.

Notice how the fireplace is raised so it can be enjoyed from various directions.

Easy Living

What makes you happy in your home? Are there things you have collected over time that reflect how you have evolved as a person . . . your tastes, your styles, your moods, your phases in life? This house is notable for its relaxed layering of detail. The color scheme is quite muted, but there is something to notice at every turn.

First, look at the structure. Classic farmhouse windows, but instead of a low ceiling, there's a high pitched ceiling and a pleasing round window at the top. The space blends old-fashioned character with a modern, almost Euro edge. Hardwood floors painted a pale gray are a great fix for floors that need a facelift and also a good way to lighten a room. You can do this with primer and any shade of porch paint. A cream color on the walls partnered with classic white trim plays up the bones of the room.

Next, notice the visual detail of the furniture. A distressed farmhouse table for a desk, French chairs upholstered in cotton duck, and a casual sofa slipcovered in white duck (note there are kids and dogs around!). The

*Curtains block the view from another room for a little privacy

*Simple roll shades are informal window treatments

*The sofa is slipcovered in washable fabric

*Paint damaged hardwood floor for an easy fix

varied pieces that are gathered together are eclectic, untraditional, and full of personality. Note there's no coffee table by the sofa. Instead, the space is left open for impromptu dancing or yoga. The desk can be used to pay bills, do homework, or play games. There are no formal window treatments, but there are roller shades for when privacy is needed. To buffer a view into the next room, a sheer floral curtain hangs on a simple curtain rod in the doorway.

One design element I love about this room is the way the family room is separated from the kitchen. The kitchen is adjacent to one end of the room, but instead of building a half-wall with the sink and countertop, the family built bookcases to serve as a dividing wall. The bookcases block the view of the kitchen from the family room and serve as a functional, stylish way to show off books. They could also hold storage baskets—a great idea that could serve several purposes.

IDEAS
you can look for and use

Vintage pieces can work beautifully in a modern space. Do you have old finds that you can bring into your room?

I love how mirrors can really open up spaces and bounce light around. They give the illusion of more space. Can you use mirrors to your advantage? Maybe lean an oversized mirror against a wall?

How do you display your books and magazines? If they were stacked on open shelving you could style them in interesting ways. Paint the back of the shelves a fun color and you get a great contrast.

Are there old floors in your home that you could paint to give them a makeover?

Find an old sofa or a chair at a tag sale, online, or at a secondhand shop and give it a new look with a slipcover. White duck and white denim are my favorite fabrics for slipcovers.

I love when people show off art from their travels. It's okay to mix media and have black-and-white photography in one place, a watercolor landscape in another, and a vintage oil painting in another. Can you be creative with art?

Creative Ranch Renovation

Smaller-scale houses can be fun to work with because the limited space challenges you to be creative. In this typical one-level ranch-style house, the homeowners updated the 1960s-style interiors to make them modern, clean, and vibrant. I came in through what was originally the living room and is now their dining room. (See pages 114–115 for a look at this room.) From there I could see into a large sunken living room.

Here the family divided the space into different zones by constructing a curved partial wall. Along the outside walls of the room they created reading areas and a place for watching TV. On the other side of the curved wall, a leather sofa fits inside the curve and faces a Southwestern-inspired fireplace. Because the wall stops short of the ceiling and has openings punched through for display, it preserves the room's feeling of openness while defining a more intimate area for conversation and relaxation. This idea for managing space would also work well in a large great room.

*A reading area is tucked behind the curved wall

IDEAS
you can look for and use

Notice the openings in the divider wall to allow light through the space. Are there ways you could create openings in your space to gain natural light and an open flow?

Simple lighting really warms things up. Halogen lights in the top of the partial wall spotlight the objects on the glass shelves below. A system of tiny spotlights sus-pended from cables mounted on the rafters sculpt the space with light. This type of lighting lets you draw attention to a piece of artwork, a seating area, or other features you want to emphasize.

Glass shelves in the built-in bookcases allow the light from above to shine down and through to illuminate objects you display.

Wood adds an organic feel. The mix of the wall finish, the wood tones of the beams above, and the finish on the wood floors gives the room an eco-friendly edge and a calm feel. Think about creative ways to use wood in your own home.

Can you add a window seat? In a smaller home, a window seat can be a space-saving way to work in extra seating and become a focal point of the room. If you can make it long enough and deep enough, like this one, it can also serve as a guest bed (or a nice place for a nap).

*A clerestory window lets in more natural light

*Openings in the wall allow air and light to flow

TV Central

Family rooms usually accommodate watching TV and playing video games. In some cases the TV becomes the focus of the room and may even overpower it.

Fortunately, many furniture companies have designed storage pieces that offer stylish solutions for the TV and its many components. Flat-screen TVs are easy to incorporate into cabinets or consoles or to hang on the wall without overwhelming the room.

Having the television out in the open is fine as long as it blends into the room. In the case of this room, a solid cabinet allows the flat-screen TV to be part of the furnishings, yet be completely visible for watching. Placement of the TV depends on where the cable connection comes in, where electrical outlets are, and available wall space. Here the staircase wall offered the only space large enough for the cabinet.

Here's an interesting thing about focal points in this room. As you come down the stairs, the fireplace is the first thing you see—clean, simple, and classic. When I first went to this house, however, the sofa was positioned in front of the French doors opposite the TV. Perfect for TV viewing, right? But it ignored the French doors and the garden outside, and also downplayed the room's natural anchor, the fireplace. So I started moving furniture around.

Now the sofa faces the fireplace, which subtly communicates ideas of warmth and gathering. The TV is still visible but doesn't dominate the space. Great natural light and inviting views through the French doors extend the sense of openness and bring the outdoors inside.

*A large hutch integrates the TV into the room

*Furniture arrangement focuses on the fireplace but allows clear views of the TV

IDEAS
you can look for and use

Neutral tones on the walls allow for colorful accessories. Neutral tones can lighten up spaces. How is your wall color treating you?

If you are going to paint your room, I suggest painting sample squares of the colors on the wall. You need to see the paint hues under different kinds of light, from daylight to evening lamp light.

Can you change your furniture around to create a new vantage point?

To carve out a smaller seating area, the sofa could be moved forward a bit, making room for a console table with some lamps. Adding electrical outlets in the floor in the center of the room gives you more options for "floating" furniture arrangements and getting lamplight into the center of the room.

Staircases are a great place to display framed family photos. Where do you show off your family?

Living with Art

Design evolves over time. That is as it should be. Rooms should grow with you as your tastes and styles change. The rustic wall finish could seem dated, but a comfortable sofa covered in cotton duck and an abstract landscape painting bring the room forward in time to a look of casual comfort. The wood tones continue along the hallway, where flagstone flooring emphasizes an organic, back-to-nature feeling. Bookcases line the hallway and a bench invites you to sit and read awhile.

Rooms should grow with you as your tastes and styles change.

Being a painter, I am always drawn to landscapes in oil, watercolor, or even just pencil. Artwork is something you acquire over time. You travel, you find things that you respond to. You may buy them on a whim with no idea of where they will end up in your home, but you just love them. Maybe a painting holds a special memory for you, or the artist was a family member, or it's one you created yourself. Whatever the source, art brings personality and life to spaces. So do books stacked on shelves and layered with photos, children's art projects, and travel mementos. Your rooms should reflect who you are. A house like this one tells a story.

*Artwork as a focal point to set a mood

*Light-colored, washable fabrics keep the room family friendly

*Natural rugs keep things light

IDEAS
you can look for and use

Art makes a statement in this room. Is art a big part of your home?

You don't need to have spotlights on your artwork, but make sure there is enough natural light or lamplight to illuminate the piece so you can enjoy it.

Notice how wood tones repeat throughout the house, from the paneled wall to the coffee table, sliding doors and wood trim in the hallway, and the book-lined library. Wood tones don't always have to match, but if they are similar in tone, they can help tie different spaces together and create a unified feeling.

Notice the great natural light that flows through the house, thanks to window placement and interior doors with glass panes. Could you replace a solid interior door with a French door to let more light into a dark hallway? If you want the room beyond to have some privacy, hang a sheer drapery panel on the back of the door, or look for a door with frosted-glass panes.

*Glass-pane interior doors let rooms share natural light

*Barn-style sliding doors are a good solution for tight spaces

Formal Options

The formal living room is making a comeback. In this house, you enter the foyer, and there is the living room off to the side. The room has a very calming feel to it. Certainly in evening light the room takes on warmer tones, yet by daylight it is cheery and uplifting. The color tones on the furnishings are neutral, which allows color to be introduced for a mood change—adding colorful throw pillows, changing out a lamp, adding a vibrant area rug to define the sofa area. I also like the fact that the table and chair set up in the bay window are what you see when you first approach the house from the outside. With the lamp turned on, the setting welcomes you in.

It's still common for these rooms to be saved for entertaining, while the family uses the "other" living space for everyday living, but I would encourage you to think about other options and additional functions for this room. Maybe this is where your CD player is and you listen to music here. Maybe the piano is here—great for entertaining and also for everyday practicing. Maybe you can bring in an armoire that hides a small home office. If it is the first room guests see as they enter your house, the living room should reflect who you are—and it should not go unused!

*A large mirror could eventually replace the artwork over sofa

*Change out pillows seasonally to give the room an instant new look

*Coffee table styling change easily for new focal points

*No window treatments keep the lines of the room clean and crisp

IDEAS
you can look for and use

Does your home have a formal living space like this?

How often do you use it? Could you make it more useful for everyday living by adding more functions?

Where do you go for quiet reading of the paper, or do you ever just kick back and listen to music?

If you have a small formal living room, use oversized mirrors to bounce light around and make the space feel larger and lighter.

If the room is small, you can use smaller area rugs to base the seating areas on. This visual trick makes the room feel larger.

*At night, the lamp and chair in the bay window look welcoming from outside

Kid Living

eing a dad, I know what it's like to have little ones around in the family room. The decorative objects that used to be displayed on tabletops make way for train sets, racing cars, blocks, and so on. Eventually you get the space back, but for a while many rooms get put on hold design-wise.

The most important thing about this kind of room is that it should be fun and happy.

If your family room is more about the kids and their needs, storage solutions for all those toys, art supplies, and games can accommodate their needs and yours. Cubbies with baskets for toys or big bins where everything goes at the end of the day let you clean up quickly and restore a sense of order to the room.

Because young kids tend to want to be where you are rather than in their own rooms, a family room that doubles as a play room is key. Plan the space to serve both adults and kids by creating a main seating area for the parents and dedicating another part of the room as a play area, with a small table and chairs for building or crafts and beanbag chairs for reading. The most important thing about this kind of room is that it should be fun and happy. It's a family room, with the emphasis on "family"—a place where adults as well as kids are comfortable.

*Reading books at your finger tips

*Dedicated storage space keeps kids' stuff organized and accessible

*Think about eco-friendly kids' furniture

*Pillows are a way to bring in fun colors you love

*A coffee table with rounded edges is kid-friendly.

IDEAS
you can look for and use

Are you environmentally friendly in your own home? For child health and safety as well as the health of the environment, consider eco-friendly play tables, bookcases, and chairs for the kids. Choose low-VOC paints, which meet EPA guidelines for maximum emission standards of volatile organic compounds, or opt for natural paints such as milk paint or plant- and earth-based paint formulations.

Colors do not need to be vibrant and bright for the kids, but bring in color in small accessories to tie it all in. What colors do you love? How could you introduce that favorite color into your room?

Slipcovered, washable fabrics on furniture are especially wise for family rooms. Is your furniture easy to clean?

Could your kids benefit from having their own corner in your family room?

How could you go about creating a space for them?

Spaces That Flow

Banks of windows bring the outdoors in, and leaving them bare emphasizes the traditional architecture and makes the most of natural light. This is a great example of a house with no formal living space but plenty of family gathering space.

This is the kind of room that can grow over time. There are great basics and bones to begin with, but the owners can add layers if they want—draperies or shades to soften the windows, new throw pillows and covers on the window seat, maybe slipcovers on the seating for a different look. With good basics, a room can easily be refreshed as the budget allows, but in the meantime it's comfortable and pleasing just as it is.

*Built-in cabinetry hides the TV and provides storage

*Great moldings and trim add richness

*Note the raised hearth for the fireplace

*A window seat built out from the wall offers extra seating for a crowd

*A table behind the sofa doubles as a desk and divides the seating areas

*Half wall and columns define the dining area

IDEAS

you can look for and use

Traditionally, window seats are built into niches or nooks in the wall, but notice how this window seat is built out from the wall. This would be an easy feature to add to an ordinary room by custom-building end tables or storage cabinets connected by a bench. The bench portion can provide additional storage. Do you have an area where you could put a window seat?

The moldings and mantel define this fireplace surround as classic in style, but it's clean-lined enough to work with transitional and more modern furnishings.

Simple changes to accessories and furniture arrangement could give this room a whole new look. How flexible is your space? Could new pillows, new lamps, and a new furniture arrangement make your family room feel like a new space?

This room works beautifully with bare windows, but imagine how it would look with tailored Roman shades or woven blinds. Draperies in the dining room would add a more formal feeling to that space. You could use different treatments in the living and dining areas and still have them relate to one another by using the same fabric in two different treatments or different fabrics in the same colors.

Trim can be painted a lighter color than the walls or stained a darker color than the walls. I like white moldings and trim, but painting trim a lighter shade of the wall color can also be attractive. The less contrast between wall color and trim work, the less attention you call to the architectural features and divisions of space. This can help a small space seem larger.

You can use the fact that you don't have crown molding to your advantage. In rooms with high ceilings, painting the ceiling the same color as the walls downplays the height of the ceiling and gives the room a more intimate feel. The absence of crown molding means you don't notice where the wall and ceiling meet, and the envelope of color can flow without obstruction.

CREATIVE
thoughts

Still more things that caught my behind-the-camera eye . . .

1 Shelves let you create visuals that can change when your mood does. Display books you love, framed photos, or old toys from when you were a kid. Change the display from time to time to keep things interesting.

2 Don't be afraid to mix and match fabrics in solids and prints. Mix textures too, if the fabrics are all in the same color family.

3 Introduce color with art, accessories, pillows, books, and so on. Sometimes art can inspire color for the rest of the room.

4 Mix up wall finishes . . . wood with painted walls, wallpaper with stone, and so on.

5 Collections are a great way of putting your own stamp on a space. Books are one of my favorites, especially old ones.

6 Photos are a way to make it feel like your space. Everyone has tons of digital family photos—print them, frame them, and display them as art!

7 Create a getaway spot for yourself. By the fire is one of my favorite spots. What spot do you love?

8 Indulge in simple treats. Cut a flower from the garden or buy yourself a bunch of tulips from the market. Treat yourself to a moment of beauty!

9 Gather stuff you love by the phone—a favorite painting, a fun mug, fun props that you respond to.

10 Lamps with a glass base are great for displaying things you love. This one is filled with shells, but you could use family photos, vintage toys, fake fruit . . . something new every season.

11 Mix it up. Throw pillows bring in style and layers. You can mix patterns while keeping an undercurrent of the same color.

HOW *to begin?*

Is your family room being good to you? If not, maybe it's time for a change. Ask yourself these questions:

Are you loving your space now? Are you not loving it? Why? Write down your answers.

What about creating a Look Book page of your dream family room? Gather some magazines tonight and tear images out when you are watching TV. By the end of the night, have a collage of images of your dream room.

Is there a living family room that you loved from a movie or TV show?

Is your basic room furniture good and something you can be creative with?

If you want new furniture, do you prefer a sectional sofa or a separate sofa and chairs? Maybe a sofa and loveseat? Think about how you want to use the room. For watching TV? Listening to music? Reading? Relaxing? Entertaining?

If you only painted the walls and added some basic new accessories, would your room have a better feel?

Could you move the furniture around and try new layouts? This is a fun Friday night thing to do.

Is that sofa up against the wall? Could you create a seating area in the middle of the room?

Could you have two seating areas in the same room? Maybe one anchored by the fireplace and another smaller one somewhere else?

How are your floors? Do you have wall-to-wall carpeting with hardwood under it? Could the hardwood be sanded and stained, or do you prefer painted floors for a new look?

If there is a TV, is it blending into the room nicely? Or is it the first thing you see when you walk in? Is it a flat screen that can be hung on the wall? Tucked inside a cabinet? Is it time to upgrade to a streamlined-looking model?

Do you want a theme for the space? Beach house? English cottage? Old Hollywood? Modern loft?

Will pets and kids be in the space? If so, what kind of fabrics can you live with?

Do you have enough storage for games, toys, DVDs, and so on?

Can you bring in items from other rooms of your house—lamps, dressers that can be used as consoles, old bedside tables for end tables, extra chairs from the guest room for a seating nook, old breakfast table for a games table? Using what you already have in new ways is a great way to save money!

Where will the Christmas tree go? Can you change the room around easily or remove something to allow for the tree?

Can you create a floor plan that will allow you to be flexible? Try moving furniture around every few months—it's a good way to change the energy!

chapter 6

Everyday Kitchens

No matter how big or small your kitchen is, it's probably the place everyone gravitates to. Whether you are entertaining your own family or a group of friends, the kitchen becomes the place to be. I find that one's idea of what a kitchen should be comes from memories of preparing or sharing meals. It is not only the center of the home for most of us, but also the center of many of our good memories of what home means.

It's amazing how food and aromas trigger those memories and thoughts. The heart-warming smells of a Thanksgiving meal being cooked bring back memories of huge family gatherings. The aroma of an apple pie baking triggers the memory of going out to pick apples and then coming home to make a pie. Fresh coffee brewing can remind you of that Sunday morning during last year's storm and how comforting it was to be safe indoors. The smell of Christmas cookies in the oven recalls the ones you bake with the kids every year. In our house the memory-maker is our traditional eggnog cake. We prepare the cake together, and the smell emanates throughout the whole house as it bakes. Then we get to enjoy it gathered around the table or the kitchen island.

My own memories of kitchens as I grew up were from those houses I visited every day after school. Though I remember some details, I recall what each kitchen smelled like and what it evoked more than anything else: the smell of a just-baked pie cooling on the window ledge, or freshly brewed tea steaming. My love of chocolate chip cookies comes from that time; the scent of baking chocolate instantly transports me back to my childhood, to that simple joy of cookies and milk and knowing that school was done for the day. As I got older, of course, I started to notice how and what made kitchen spaces really work.

Finding Your Style

So with that in mind, the question becomes, what mood or feeling do you want your kitchen to convey? You can have a wonderful space with great stuff in it, but if it doesn't convey a feeling or invite you in, then what is the point? To me that emotional charge inspires the look and direction for your style.

If you want a kitchen that spells out comfort and warmth, you might like a country style with warm wood tones, distressed furniture, faded fabrics, and antique collections. Bowls of fruit, baking items gathered within easy reach, and big cutting boards ready to prepare a feast all say "welcome home." At the other end of the spectrum, maybe you can't stand clutter. You like clean lines and only a few things left out on countertops and tables. Take a

The kitchen is not only the center of the home,
but also the center of good memories of what home means.

modern black-and-white loft, for example. It's sleek in design with a Euro edge to it. Dim the lights, turn up the jazz music, and you have a welcoming environment in which to entertain your friends. Both places say "welcome home" even though they look and feel very different, because they express the personalities of the people who live in them. The film *The Holiday* captures these contrasting styles. One of the kitchens is very country cottage with lots of layers of details, while the other is sleek and simple, conveying a more modern way of designing a kitchen.

Personally, I like several different looks. A minimalist, modern kitchen with white or stainless base cabinets, concrete countertops, and open upper shelves displaying all-white dishware satisfies my need to have things in order. With nothing on the counter besides an elegant flower arrangement, this type of kitchen makes me feel that I have room to move around, and my mind doesn't feel crowded by things bombarding me visually. This is something you might want to think about in your own home.

Do you like returning to your desk in the morning with everything in order? Are you the kind of person who won't go to bed without washing the dishes, giving you a clean slate for the next day? I think that people who live in modern spaces like the efficiency of clean lines and uncluttered living because it suits their mindset. It lets them focus on other things, and the upkeep of the spaces is easy.

On the flip side, I love a country house with lots of layering of things—textures, colors, details, art, collections, pieces acquired over time. The layered, more lived-in look satisfies my need for having a comforting, nurturing environment around me. Things that I love are in sight and can be enjoyed. There may be more things going on visually than in a minimalist environment, but that can be uplifting and inviting.

Some kitchens are specifically designed for those who love to cook, while others are obviously for those who use their kitchen for eating takeout and reading the Sunday paper. Even a kitchen that you are living with "for now," saving up for a renovation, still needs to work for your daily life. Renovating a kitchen can be expensive, but you don't have to break the bank to make your kitchen work for you. There are creative solutions that can transform it easily and beautifully. The important thing to focus on is that in everyday life you need to surround yourself with environments that make you feel good. And so begins the process of figuring out what works for you.

What is the style of your current kitchen? How do you feel when you walk into it? When you walked into a friend's new kitchen or you saw a great kitchen when you were looking for a new house, what did that space feel like? What resonated with you and why?

Making Your Space Work for You

It's a myth that you must have a huge kitchen to have the kitchen of your dreams. One of my first projects was in a New York City apartment. It had an old Pullman kitchen that was hidden in a closet. To turn it into an attractive, usable space, I removed the closet doors and installed an all-in-one stainless-steel unit with a sink, under-counter fridge, four-burner range, and an oven. Above the unit, I hung white open shelving with simple brackets to store and display white dinnerware and glassware. The open shelving served a function—storage for food, supplies, and plates—but it also looked great because items were arranged in an appealing way. You can do this too—think matching storage containers for pastas and cookies, attractive bottles and cans of food and drink, classic dishware—simple and clean.

For added counter space, I brought in a large stainless-steel island with a big work area on top and a shelf underneath for stainless pots and cookware. Matching stools from a restaurant wholesale supply store finished off the area and provided seating. The look was modern, yet it worked well with a comfortable and inviting living room, which was in the same area.

The kitchen can be the most challenging room to renovate, but it does not have to be as stressful as you might imagine. Focus on the feeling you want to have for your space.

When you are beginning the makeover process, whether it's a large job or a small one, keep the essence of what you are trying to create in your mind's eye. Choosing products and details can be overwhelming, but to keep from being paralyzed by indecision, focus on the feeling you want to have for *your* space. Imagine yourself in your finished kitchen having your morning coffee, entertaining friends, or making dinner with your family. That mental picture will help guide you through the process, help you make decisions on products or accessories, and keep you focused on the steps toward your goal. The Look Book will also help you stay focused on your overall vision for the space, and it will help you communicate that clearly to contractors and subcontractors. The kitchen involves many products and components so it can be the most challenging room to renovate, but it does not have to be as stressful as you might imagine. Pace yourself and take it step by step.

The following pages show real-life families in their kitchen environments. As you look at them, notice what you are drawn to. Circle, highlight, and make notes where you see fit on these pages. You will see how much of a designer you truly are—the key is to follow your instincts and stick with them. As with your Look Book pages, you'll start to notice what you like or are drawn to. Recognizing that is how you begin to figure it all out for yourself.

Down-Home Style

To me this is the ultimate American family preparing a summer dinner at home. They represent what a kitchen should be: a gathering space where people spend time together and reconnect as a family. The kitchen is not high-end in terms of products, but it captures the essence of a family setting that works. I remember distinctly what it felt like to walk into that space: welcoming and peaceful.

There are not many cabinets, but what's there is efficient and of good quality. The old farmhouse sink adds great character, and it's handsome as well as functional. The appliances are good, traditional appliances that serve the family's needs. The windows have perfect, classic lines, and leaving them uncovered emphasizes the clean look while letting in the maximum amount of light. The style is very New England farmhouse. Gathering the cookbooks in one area creates an inviting look that says, "Come in, pick a recipe, and start cooking!"

My favorite thing about the space is the openness of the farmhouse floor plan. The kitchen work area flows into the eating area (not shown), so the whole space is casual and inviting. In the cooking area, the wood finish on the work surfaces adds warmth, as does the earthy color of the tile floor. The cream color of the painted cabinets and walls makes the room feel light and bright. There is no clutter, and everything serves a purpose. Clean, simple, and efficient.

As a designer, I love this kitchen because I immediately felt at home in this space. It reminded me of that old TV show *The Waltons:* a classic-style kitchen that has character and welcomes you in. I can imagine these girls coming home from college to this kitchen and talking with their mom and dad about their adventures. That is how kitchens find themselves very much a part of our life moments.

*Uncovered windows let in the maximum amount of light

*An old farmhouse sink adds character

*Wood counters add to the warm feel

*Recessed ceiling lights give overall illumination

*Tile floor is easy to clean

*Note storage in the side of the island

IDEAS

you can look for and use

Do you have a vintage home that has character like this one? What could you do to bring out that character?

If you don't have an old home, can you install a vintage sink or materials from an architectural salvage company to add character? If you are building a home, can you be creative with the details and layout to achieve the welcoming, casual feeling this kitchen has?

How do you like working and entertaining in your space now? Does this open plan appeal to you, or do you like separate, more intimate areas for prep, eating, and conversation?

Could you turn a large closet near your kitchen into a big walk-in pantry for all your food storage and extra kitchenware? That could mean you'd need fewer cabinets, so you could devote more wall space to windows for views and light.

Are you drawn to this uncluttered look? Does it make you realize that you have too much stuff going on in your own kitchen?

Do you spend time preparing meals as a family, or are you always rushing? Can you make a point of preparing a meal together and sharing one a few times a week? Whatever happened to the old tradition of Sunday dinners being special? It's time to revive that custom.

—Beachless Beach House Getaway—

This kitchen was originally very small, probably untouched since the 1960s. When this family bought the house, they knew the kitchen wouldn't always work for them, but other things took priority on their to-do list. When they couldn't live with the space any more, they had to decide whether to do a simple redesign within the existing footprint or expand the room with a larger addition. Finally, they decided to make it their dream kitchen as part of a larger renovation. But they had a hard time verbalizing what the dream would look like. As it turned out, the movie *Something's Gotta Give* with Diane Keaton helped them pinpoint the mood they were after. I knew they wanted a beach house look, and that film had a great example, so I suggested they watch it. The kitchen inspired them and helped them communicate what they were drawn to. Although we didn't copy the film set, we used it to generate a direction for the renovation.

The homeowners were clear about certain things: They wanted stainless-steel appliances, more work space and countertop areas, and an open floor plan. Inspired by the movie kitchen set, I chose white cabinets, stainless-steel appliances, and an earth-friendly stone product for the countertops. The windows look like double-hung windows but are actually casements to let in as much natural light as possible yet retain a classic look. To get the casual but traditional feeling they wanted, I chose a more expensive, higher-end cabinetry that resembles built-in furniture. You can certainly be creative with less costly cabinets and achieve a high-end, stylish look with lighting, flooring, and accents. In this case, however, because the room was an open plan, the cabinets would play a major role in defining the style. Function (such as drawers closing automatically), accent trim, and finishing details mean you get what you pay for in quality cabinets. The details made what could have been boring white cabinets much more impressive visually. And because the cabinets line up mainly on one wall, fewer units were needed. To balance the cost of the cabinetry, I opted for a budget-friendly line of stainless-steel appliances instead of more expensive ones. Stainless steel gives a restaurant-inspired look that works well with the high-end cabinetry and provides contrast to all the white woodwork for a more interesting look.

Unlike the old space, this new, open room made me feel like the beach was right outside, instead of hours away. Design can transport you to new places. Where do you want to be transported?

*The countertops are made from an earth-friendly stone product

*Under-cabinet lights provide task lighting

*Storage on both sides of island

*The cabinetry resembles built-in furniture

BEFORE

*Frosted glass doors let in-cabinet lighting glow but hide contents

IDEAS

you can look for and use

Notice the lighting and how it's layered. Lighting brings life to a room. Pendant lights, in-cabinet, under-cabinet, and ceiling lights all play a role in creating the mood you want. Lighting serves various purposes in kitchens: ambient overall light, task and focal light for prep, and decorative lights for sparkle. Are there things you can do with lighting in your current space to improve its function and mood?

An island provides another work surface and a new dimension to the space, whether you have room for a big central work island like this one, with seating for guests, or you have room for only a small butcher-block rolling cart. Can an island be incorporated into your kitchen?

Notice how the upper cabinets by the gas range are not set flush—some of the units are deeper than others. Simple tricks like breaking up a bank of cabinets can add richness and interest.

Also notice the various types of cabinets—glass front, solid door, long doors for larger storage, cubby drawers, and pot drawers. Storage is key in any kitchen, but a solid wall of cabinet doors and drawers can close in a space or feel too uniform. Can you mix it up a bit in your own space? How much storage do you actually need?

Cabinets that look like pieces of furniture can give a kitchen an individual, collected-over-time look. You can create the effect using standard cabinets, moldings, trim, and countertops. Is that a look you like?

Do you have a good work triangle in your kitchen? Traditionally, the sink, stove, and fridge should form a triangle for the easiest workflow and greatest efficiency. If you don't have that in your space now, think about ways to make the workflow smoother.

The sink is mounted under the counter, which makes countertop cleanup easy (see bottom-right photo on page 86). The sleek lines and brushed-metal finish of the sink and faucet add a nice, clean look to the kitchen. Could you change out your sink or faucet to give your kitchen a quick makeover?

Flooring needs to be practical for maintenance; durable for pets, kids, and heavy traffic; and comfortable to stand on. I like ceramic tile (with radiant heating under it) and hardwood, but for this kitchen I chose an eco-friendly laminate that looks like vintage barn board. If you want to bring green products into your home, flooring is a good way to do it, either with new products or with salvaged, repurposed hardwoods.

Vintage Comes Home Again

When I walked into this kitchen, I was drawn to the details. It is an older home with some of the original built-ins, but it also has the feeling of a space that has evolved over time with a growing family. I would label it an eclectic space because vintage pieces have been brought in to add character and style, yet it's a functional, everyday kitchen. The pot rack above the window, the bake ware hung like art on the walls, and the mixing of props add layers, yet are simple items used in creative ways. There is very little counter space and prep area, so the family is creative with what they have. The wall with the built-in hutch inspires the wood tones carried through to the table and chairs. Glass doors and open shelves on the hutch allow the family to show off collections that add more visual interest and detail. If they wanted to change the look of this area instantly, they could paint the inside walls of the hutch to brighten it up while keeping the outside surfaces stained. New dishware inside would give it a whole new look, too.

One thing that keeps the kitchen fun is the use of period pieces. The light fixture, for example, is a reminder of a time gone by, and the vintage cabinet over the counter area brings in a certain style and depth. Period detail does not have to mean living in a museum; it can add charm and character to a new house, too. Architectural salvage shops sell moldings, cabinets, banisters, windows, mantels, and other items saved from old houses and commercial buildings that have been torn down. Although originally marketed to people who were restoring old houses, these items are perfect for repurposing in new homes. The craftsmanship and patina of old pieces that have been well-loved through the decades gives them a unique character all their own. This is definitely a kitchen you'd come home to after school and have some cookies and milk. Note those cookies on the counter (subliminal advertising).

*The pot rack is a functional storage solution

*Could add open shelving (where clock area is) if more storage were needed

*Plenty of outlets make the small prep space functional

*Paneled doors say vintage country style

*A built-in hutch supplies great storage

IDEAS

you can look for and use

The wood of the built-ins is rich and warm. But if you wanted to go lighter for a new look, you could easily prime and paint your wood cabinets. Or add a pop of color to the interior of a glass-front cabinet to make a creative statement.

Vintage lighting like the pendant over the table adds character. Could you find an old lamp and have it rewired to use as a chandelier? Check salvage shops and lamp stores for fixtures that have been saved from old houses and rewired. It's a great way to add character and style to a new space.

This kitchen has only one small area for food prep—where the wall cabinets are. When the family needs more room for meal preparation and baking, the kitchen table becomes an extension of the work space. How can you make the most of your own space?

If you have limited room, look for a pot rack that mounts above the window—it takes advantage of underused space and doesn't block the light.

Updated Living

Originally this kitchen had dark green cabinets, and the appliances were dated, dark, and rustic. The family was ready for a change, but instead of a complete overhaul, they decided to be creative with what they had. By priming and painting the cabinets a light neutral color and painting the walls a darker muted tone, they changed the look to one that's fresh and elegant. New hardware and pulls also upgraded the cabinets. Finally, they replaced their existing appliances with sleek stainless-steel and black ones and added a new, contemporary dining table and chairs.

This kitchen is a good example of a variation on the work triangle layout. The cooktop is in the island opposite the sink, so filling pots with water or putting dirty pans in the sink is convenient. The wall oven and microwave are within easy reach at one end of the island, and the refrigerator is at the other end. Two or more people can work together in this kitchen and not get in each other's way. And having the cooktop in the center allows the host to enjoy prepping while still being able to connect with guests. (Instead of an overhead exhaust vent, the range has a disappearing vent that pops up along the back edge.)

Other changes that could be made over time here include adding new pendant lights over the work island, changing out the countertops and backsplash, and installing a new island counter with an overhang to accommodate stools.

Another thing I like about this kitchen is that the table is right beside the main kitchen area. Although the family has a formal dining room, this is where they eat their daily meals. This kind of open layout can be a challenge for homeowners who want to use different paint colors in the two spaces—where do you stop one color and start another? In this room, the color on the cabinets carries over to the trim and moldings as well as the fireplace mantel. The trim color provides a foundation that unifies the room.

*Existing cabinets were primed and painted for a fresh look

*Instead of an overhead exhaust vent, a vent pops up along the back edge of the range.

IDEAS

you can look for and use

Can you prime and paint your cabinets to update your kitchen? Paint can make such a dramatic difference. Another option here would be removing some of the doors on upper cabinets to create open storage.

Would changing your countertops give your kitchen a better look? In this kitchen there are tile countertops and the center island has warm wood; countertops are a chance to mix surfaces and be creative.

What's the view outside your window now? Could you plant trees or shrubs to create a better view or screen the view of a neighbor's house?

Wood floors or tile? This kitchen has great rustic wood floors that were refinished to clean and shine them up, adding a layer of richness to the room. Having all wood cabinets matched with wood floors would have made wood too overpowering, but with painted cabinets, the floors literally shine as the wood accent in the room. In thinking of flooring for your own space, ask yourself how much maintenance you want to do. For example, wood floors can get scratched by pets, and darker stained wood floors show more dirt. If you choose tile, think about how cold the floor may feel in the winter months. You might want to consider radiant heat under the tile to keep it warmer.

Stainless-steel appliances look high-end and professional, but they're not magnet-friendly. If you like putting up soccer schedules, yoga postcards, report cards, and family photos on your fridge, stainless steel may not be for you. But if you love the look of stainless and you need a message center too, think about hanging an oversized chalkboard on a wall. Or try painting part of your wall with magnetic paint for an instant message board. I love how this kitchen has bookcases above the kitchen desk, but I could also see a message board placed here. I have also seen backsplashes

made from magnetic boards so that things can be displayed things with magnets. You could even take it one step further and paint one whole wall with black chalkboard paint for a functional and decorative message board.

What everyday appliances do you need on your countertops? Do you like having everything out in the open or do you prefer things stored away? In this kitchen, most things are out of sight. Freeing up countertops enables you to put out decorative props, establish a theme, or accent your room.

Do you need a desk in your kitchen—a place to do bills, sort through recipes, check messages, work on your laptop, and so on? Having a desk in the kitchen works for some families, but for others it ends up being a catch-all for clutter. What about for you? Here, having the long eating table close by serves as a desk for the kids to do homework and be with the family while meal prep is going on.

If you don't have an open kitchen plan, do you have a way of creating a breakfast area or nook? Whether it's a bar with stools or a corner with a small table, bench, and chairs, what can you create? For example, if this family used their regular dining room for everyday meals, they could have a series of stools at the island counter and bring in comfortable chairs to create a seating area with an ottoman where the long table is now.

*Desk nook organizes cookbooks and home-office tasks

Modern Family Style

This kitchen, in an ordinary suburban home, is a great example of transitioning from traditional style to modern. Although the layout is not exactly the same as the previous kitchen, there are similarities—the bar area, the adjoining dining area, big windows over the sink—so you can see how the same basic structure can go in an entirely different direction.

This space is a fine example of mixing finishes and having it work to your advantage. Dark and light tones mesh to create the illusion of more space and a pleasant, modern surprise. White cabinets with a glass-tile backsplash and polished black countertops put a contemporary spin on the room. A basic, classic stovetop partnered with a more streamlined vent hood takes the look to a new level. Even something as simple as drawer and cabinet hardware can make an impact. A more traditional knob style would have been safe, but the long, sleek handles are clean and contemporary, giving the space a hipper vibe.

The wall of darker cabinetry with stainless appliances becomes like a wall of built-in furniture and adds richness to the room. Filling the kitchen with dark wood tones would have made it seem smaller. Mixing various finishes creates the feel of more space.

*Note the different finishes used on the countertops and cabinetry

*Lighting emphasizes modern style

*Metal-and-plastic chairs are practical, durable, and modern.

*Carpet tiles for easy care

*Glass tiles pull together the contrasting light and dark tones

*Contemporary door handles update traditional cabinets

*Streamlined stove exhaust hood

IDEAS
you can look for and use

The cabinets are mixed, with solid white on one side and dark walnut on the other side. This balancing act between different finishes and styles creates a sophisticated, high-contrast look that opens up the sense of space. Is this something you could do and use to your advantage in your space?

Want to express your own personal style? Decorative hardware for cabinets and drawers offers you many options. What do you like? A knob or pull with a leaf motif could play up a natural theme, or something more dramatic could make the hardware a focal point.

Backsplashes add color, texture, and style. Tile and paint are popular options. Stainless-steel sheets or tiles give a restaurant-style look. The thin, horizontal glass tiles in this kitchen, with their neutral color and random pattern, emphasize a modern feel. What do you like?

Choosing a modern look for the pendant lights gives the whole room a new feel. Note the mix of glass pendants over the bar area with a classic drum shade over the eating area. Decorative lighting creates focal points that draw the eye in. Under-cabinet lighting adds task lighting for meal prep but can be dimmed for mood lighting when eating or entertaining.

Dining furniture completes the modern upgrade. The table's straight lines and simplicity suggest Shaker-style furniture, so it could just as easily partner with ladder-back chairs for a country look. But add contemporary plastic stacking chairs, and the table becomes part of the new modern look. Is this something you could do in your kitchen? A new table, chairs, and even bar stools can refresh a room. The bar stools don't have to match the table and chairs. You could use modern metal stools that harmonize, or choose a style that contrasts with the style of the chairs.

Carpet squares under the table create a foundation for the eating area and bring the colors of the room to the floor. They're functional if you have kids and pets because individual squares can be removed and cleaned. Do you need to have an area rug under your table? No, but it adds a layer to break up the open floor plan and creates a "moment," defining the area.

*The lighting helps to create a homey atmosphere

PANTRY

*These cabinets were painted green to look like an old built-in hutch

The Gathering

This farmhouse kitchen is probably one of my favorite kitchens because it looks like a vintage farmhouse space yet is in a newly built house. Its details, levels of light, and views to the outside all help create a mood that says there truly is no place like home.

When I first walked into this home, we were there to shoot a television show and I fell in love with how it was put together. I found myself constantly turning around and finding something new to discover.

Mixing different finishes and styles of cabinets, countertop surfaces, and details can be a creative way to bring a room to life and give it an unfitted, collected-over-time feeling. Here, cabinets on the left side of the room have been painted green to look like an old hutch, while the rest of the cabinets are white. Although these are all new pieces, you could get the same effect with vintage or repurposed cabinets. It's also a good way to work with what you have and make it better. For example, instead of replacing all of your cabinets, bring in some stand-alone pieces that work with your old cabinets but give the

kitchen a fresh style. You could use an old armoire, a hutch, or even an old dresser as part of your scheme.

The fun part of this space is that it feels intimate yet is open to other areas—the pantry, the formal dining room beyond the opening above the gas range, and, through the windows, the garden. The openness creates a flow of energy. The large central island enables one person to prep on one side, another to do a project or homework on the other side, and others to help out without getting in each other's way. I can attest to this because I was in there with a TV crew and equipment, and it still worked!

This kitchen also uses lighting well. The schoolhouse pendants over the island, the under-cabinet lights, the interesting wall sconces by the range, and the recessed lights in the ceiling can be controlled individually to provide the right combination of task and mood lighting for any activity. No matter how well you design or redesign a space, it does not truly come to life until it is properly lit. A good lighting plan balances practical function, aesthetics, and mood.

IDEAS
you can look for and use

There are many options for vent hoods over ranges. What are you drawn to? Do you like a basic hood, or do you prefer one that is more customized to look like furniture? Or do you like metals such as copper or brushed nickel?

This kitchen has an extra room for a pantry for food, baking items, an extra prep sink, a freezer, a home office area, a recycling area, and a bulletin board for messages. Could you create a space like this? If you have a closet off your kitchen or in the mudroom nearby, could you transform it into a pantry area? Is there another spot in the house—perhaps the garage—where you could put up open shelves for bulk supplies?

Could you live with glass-front cabinets? Some people don't like guests to see inside their messy cabinets. If you had glass doors, would you keep the items inside organized? If so, they are a nice way to display attractive dishes, bowls, crystal, or even boxes or cans of food with appealing labels.

The gas range area opens to the formal dining room beyond, giving the kitchen more depth and space. If the wall were closed up, this corner would have no natural light or view. Could you open a partial wall between your kitchen and dining area to gain a greater sense of space?

Note that the shape of the island is angled like the shape of the kitchen. Islands are a great way to add more work surface and storage. If you don't have a big space to work with, get a butcher-block rolling island. If you have a bigger space, think about how to bring in a built-in island.

*Note the wall sconce for accent and task lighting

*A pass-through connects kitchen to dining room

CREATIVE
thoughts

Here are some visuals that have inspired me. I hope they give you food for thought in your own kitchen.

1 Notice how natural light flows into your space and make the most of it. Use it to your advantage—natural light can improve your mood.

2 Your breakfast table is a place for eating, but also for sharing family time for games, homework, art projects, and conversation—all very important.

3 Even a small kitchen can have a high-end, restaurant-style look with a stainless-steel backsplash and a stainless-steel gas range with backsplash and vent hood.

4 Levels of lighting are key in any space, but especially in the kitchen. Think about how you will be using your space—you'll need task light for food prep and cleanup, but accent lights can bring the space to life and enhance the mood. Controlling the levels of light is key to creating mood—dimmers are a must-have.

5 Windows do not always have to be covered up. If yours have clean, classic lines, show them off. And a great view is like another room of your house—enjoy it!

6 Kitchens are always going to be about gathering with family and friends. A good cup of coffee, a visit from a friend, and our pets are still the simple joys in life.

7 Foods are a great visual inspiration in the kitchen. From the warmth of red apples in the fall to the bounty of veggies from the garden—enjoying food prep and good meals together are what kitchens should be about.

8 Countertops are usually the same throughout for a unified look, but think about using different materials according to the work zone. A heat-resistant stone surface beside the cooktop is practical for pans as well as baking or pasta making, while a butcher-block surface is perfect for chopping vegetables and cutting bread.

9 Many kitchens flow into other living areas. Rooms that blend together nicely invite you in from wherever you are standing.

HOW
to begin?

As you plan your kitchen (re)design, ask yourself these questions:

What do you love about your kitchen now? Write these things down.

What don't you like about your kitchen? Write these things down, too.

What is the best kitchen you have ever been in? What did it say to you? What did it feel like to be there? What did you connect to? Write that down.

A really hard question for some people to answer is how long they will be staying in the house. If you may be moving in a few years, is it worth spending a lot of money on your kitchen, or are there things you can do to make it better without breaking the budget? Perhaps this is your dream house, so you might want to make it all it can be. What's your situation?

Does your kitchen layout work now? What layout could make it work better? For example, is your sink far away from your stove? Is the fridge crammed into a corner with the door opening the wrong way? Are there too many doors into the room that take away from storage options and create too much traffic? Could closing up a doorway give you more space?

Could removing some upper cabinets make room for more windows and natural light?

What could you quickly change about your kitchen if you had to do something in one day? One week? A month? What would give you an instant change *now*?

Is your kitchen inviting and warm or cluttered and over-whelming? Is it a space you enjoying coming into and preparing a meal or entertaining friends in?

What do you think your personal style is in this space? Are you modern—stainless-steel appliances, sleek Euro-style cabinets, minimal accessories, streamlined lighting? Or are you into layered details of country style, with distressed furniture, collections on display, faded fabrics, wood accents? Or are you eclectic in your style, mixing modern with country? You don't have to label your style, but it is fun to think about what you want that result to be.

continues

Have you seen a kitchen in a magazine, in a friend's house, or even in a movie that appeals to you? Use that as a visual guide toward your goal for the space.

If you have a visual guide in mind that you are drawn to, pick that room apart. What do you love about it? Write that down. You want to begin to see the layers that you respond to so you can bring those elements to life in your own space.

Could you do a cosmetic makeover in your kitchen for under $500? Remember, a can of paint, some new hardware, some new lighting, and basic new props can make a huge difference.

If you are thinking of doing a major renovation, ask yourself, can you live without a kitchen for a while? Would this stress you out too much? Do you really need to do a major renovation and spend the money? Could that money be spent in creative ways: priming and painting existing cabinets, buying new appliances, removing tired upper cabinets and putting in open shelving, or installing a great lighting plan?

If your kitchen is new but has a generic look, can you use paint to bring life to it? How about adding a stylish backsplash to bring in depth, framing your kid's art to display on the empty walls, or painting a wall with chalkboard paint to bring real-life dimension to the room? New or generic kitchens can be a blank canvas to have fun with—so have fun!

If you are replacing cabinets, do you like dark wood cabinets or all white? How about mixing colors and finishes? There is no one right way, so do what you respond to personally.

Do you need to replace appliances? Restaurant-quality appliances have been a trend in high-end kitchen renovations, but now you can find budget-friendly stainless-steel appliances that give you the same look for less. All-white appliances offer a classic look, too.

Lighting is a big part of any redesign. What is your lighting like now? Could you add layers—under-cabinet lights, new pendant lights over an island or the sink, in-cabinet lights, or even small spot halogen lights for accent lighting? Remember, dimmers are key to controlling the levels of light and creating a mood in the space.

Look Books for kitchens are essential. Have you begun gathering images and details that can empower you and keep you focused as you begin a redesign? Start putting it together *now* for fun!

chapter 7

Dining In

The way I like to think of dining rooms is to imagine how people gather there. It can be casual and spontaneous or more formal and planned—it's not so much about the food as it is the mood that is created. The dining room is where you share conversation and happy times over meals with family and friends, creating memories and moments of celebration—anniversaries, birthdays, Christmas dinner, the first day of school. You want to make it special, and this room helps set the scene.

The houses where I grew up had separate dining rooms that were used only for special occasions. We wouldn't go into them for everyday meals, and the table became a catch-all for stuff. Today, I love to cook and I love having a dining room specifically designed for sharing meals and good times. It's still a room for special occasions—a child's birthday, a friend's adoption celebration, a romantic dinner for two, a Sunday morning brunch—but using it for everyday breakfasts or dinners as a family makes those times special, too.

The dining room is often a room in limbo—stuck in a phase or not really going anywhere. With the way many families live today—breakfast on the run, lunch at school, and dinner varying according to each person's schedule after soccer games or play dates—the dining room can seem unnecessary, like an afterthought. If you use it only at Thanksgiving, you might think, *What's the point of making it better?* If that sounds like your situation, maybe you need to step back and start thinking about your dining room in a new way. What if it could serve several purposes? What if you actually used this room every day? If it were decorated and furnished in a way you loved, would you use it more and entertain more?

As a room with no distractions of television or video games, the dining room offers you a place to put quality time back into your family's life with meals around the dinner table. It's also a room that can serve more than one purpose. I recently helped a family create a new dining room, and to make sure it wasn't used just for guest dining, I made it a library, too—bookshelves with books, a

Maybe you need to step back and start thinking about your dining room in a new way.

*Using the dining room as a library or office extends function

seating area by the fireplace, a big farmhouse table with stacks of books, a sideboard for serving ware as well as office supplies. Now in addition to being a place for meals, the room is perfect for reading a book by the fire, working from home at the big table, or letting the kids have a space for doing homework with their friends. This way, a room that usually goes unused can serve more than one purpose. Everything needs a purpose.

The dining room is truly about mood and about setting a stage.

The dining room should reflect your tastes and the way you live—don't feel like you have to use the same kind of furniture your grandmother did (or that you have to use your grandmother's furniture). Perhaps a rustic French farmhouse style with an American twist—French stainless-steel chairs around a table made of long barn boards set on industrial metal legs. Dining rooms are a great place to mix it up a bit. You can have a wooden table as the focal point and surround it with chairs in different finishes or upholstered chairs. You could even have a metal table—zinc-top tables can look industrial or rustic. Bring in mismatched vintage chairs, long benches, or church pews for an eclectic look. Instead of electric overhead lighting, you might opt for resting lanterns along the table or hanging candleholders over the table.

Think about how you see yourself in your dining room. Picture yourself in what you want your space to be. How will you use it? How will it feel? What kind of table will you have? Are you formal or more casual in style when you entertain? The Look Book will help guide you to what you want most, but I think the dining room is truly about mood and setting a stage. It's not only about food presentation and enjoying a gathering time around the table, but also about how everyone feels being in your space.

Hitting the road with my camera, I found some dining rooms with moods worth capturing. Take a look.

Fun French Style

Here is a dining room option that is simply fun—a farmhouse table made from an old barn door on sawhorse legs with black wicker end chairs and French metal chairs. I like the fact that outdoor seating has come inside and that the seating can be changed instantly to give the room a new look. Some days might call for the metal chairs, while on others you might use only wicker, with a few throw pillows added for color and comfort. A simple vintage-looking Paris factory light hangs over the table, directing light down onto food and guests. It hangs on a pulley with a weight, so it can be lowered or raised easily as needed. A sisal area rug under the seating adds a layer of warmth and texture that is easy on the eye. In the summer, the rug goes into storage and the floor stays bare for a clean, modern feeling. Everything about this space says, "Come gather." It makes me think of a scene from *Chocolat* or *Under the Tuscan Sun*. Intimacy, camaraderie, and light-heartedness. How does your scene play out? The soundtrack here would be like the soundtrack to *Chocolat*.

*Interior French doors allow rooms to flow yet be separate

*Mixed styles of seating make the room casual

*Wicker chairs can be used inside or out

*Natural rug anchors the room

IDEAS
you can look for and use

The color on the walls changes with the various light sources. Sometimes it looks like a pale green-blue and sometimes it's more gray. The right paint color in a room can really shape the mood.

Have fun with creating your own table—who says you have to have a formal, permanent dining table? Instead of sawhorses, you could use vintage iron legs from a salvage yard or even oversized garden urns.

Add a bench instead of chairs for creative seating at your table.

Instead of an electrified fixture over your table, try a chandelier with candles or votives for a softer light.

Artwork is great in any space, and you don't have to frame paintings on canvas. Simply hang the canvas on the wall. It gives a more casual, art-studio feel to the room.

Want to bring in more color, yet keep it flexible? Add throw pillows and rugs with richer colors—you can change them out easily.

To add more layers to this room, I can see adding a curtain rod and fabric panels or fabric shirred on tension rods to the French door leading to the living area beyond. Create visual interest around a door and give it style.

*Make your own dining table from a salvaged barn door and sawhorse or wrought iron base legs

Modern Living

This open-plan dining area, which flows into the kitchen and out to the yard, is a perfect example of modern family living. The space is easy on the eye, with a mix of rustic and modern. It has different moods—by day, it's bright and sunny, vacationlike. By evening light, its colors are warm, and the space invites lingering. Looking at rooms at different times of day is almost like looking at a movie set. The daytime reveals the great outdoors, and the colors of nature become part of the design mood. Then, by night, the backdrop is gone and the room comes alive on its own in a whole new way. Look at your room in the daylight and evening light. What do you see?

The clean, classic white window trim makes the architecture of the windows and doors stand out. This house shows how important windows are, not only to the exterior architectural character of your house, but also to the way you decorate the interiors. With no window treatments, the lines of the windows make the statement. For more color in the room, I could easily see Roman shades being added, with colors stemming from those in the throw pillows. Or 2-inch wooden blinds could be installed inside the window frame to control light and privacy without covering the trim molding. Blinds are also a good way to obscure an ugly view or your neighbor's kitchen window!

Notice how the table is off to the side, creating a non-traditional table layout. This leaves the path to the French doors clear. The table is wood tone and the chairs are black. Mixing pieces creates a more casual feel. A built-in bench or banquette is a solution for seating and also for storage needs (your outdoor cushions for patio furniture could be stashed there, or all those board games you'll be playing on Friday nights). With neutral room colors it's up to the layering of striped and patterned fabrics to bring in splashes of color. Adding a red or yellow pillow would change the color mood if desired.

This is a great space for everyday meals with the family. Get some fun dishware, add some seashells, some music, and transport yourself to your favorite getaway spot every day. It all seems to say: Take the time to enjoy the simple things—family, friends, and good food.

If the dining room is a stage set for celebrating family and friends, what might the soundtrack for this room be? *Something's Gotta Give*, of course!

*The table is off to one side in a non-traditional layout

*Classic white trim makes the windows and doors stand out

IDEAS

you can look for and use

Instead of having a dining table with chairs, could you save space with a long bench or a built-in window seat like this one? It's a great way to bring in softer items like the seat cushion and throw pillows.

Do you have to have window treatments? If your yard or view is private, what about saving some money and keeping the windows bare?

Could you use an area rug under your table? The rug defines the seating area, but if you have kids who are a bit messy during meals, you might omit that for awhile. Put furniture pads on the chair feet to make moving chairs easier. Or consider changing the rug with the seasons—sisal or bare floors for summer, something dark-colored and warm for winter.

This room had space for French doors that open into the room. If you don't have that much space, you could install a single French door flanked by two windows. Or you could have doors that open out to save on inside space.

I like lighting that can be directed down on the table. That way the whole room is not washed with the light over the table. Dimmers are good here.

Bear in mind that installing pendants or a chandelier over the dining table locks you into a certain table placement. If there were no pendants over this table, it could be pulled out into the room with chairs placed around it. The built-in bench would become a window seat.

Notice the finish on the table and chairs. The black accents really stand out against the paler wall tones and white trim. White chairs could have been used here, but the black anchors the space visually.

Family Life

Dining rooms can become a place for traditions to begin, for everyday rituals that become part of the tapestry of your family life. Simple moments like setting the table for dinner, mother and daughter laughing and sharing the stories of their day. It's nothing extraordinary, yet it is so powerful.

The wonderful thing about this space is that it's convenient to the kitchen and is used for both everyday meals and special occasions. Why not light candles for everyday meals or gather a bunch of flowers? Do things that make you happy.

What makes this all work is that there is a great mix of personality pieces: The modern farmhouse table with trim-lined chairs for an up-to-date look combines with a large vintage hutch. It's a good example of how rooms can grow over time and how the layering of acquired things gives a room emotional depth and richness. The vintage piece might have been one you loved at the antiques market years ago, so you bought it and stored it until you could use it. Now you have a place for it, but your tastes have evolved and you want something more modern. So as you buy new pieces you begin to show signs of your newfound self. All of that is okay because it is you. Remember, where are *you* in all this?

The other point about mixing personality pieces is that it's a way for couples to combine their styles, which works especially well in dining rooms. This is where your Look Book comes in. Each of you should gather images of what you love and have a meeting of creative minds to find mutual ground. Get creative together to make a space you both love being in.

You can't go wrong with white dinnerware because you can embellish it as you set your table for various occasions.

One last lesson from this house: If you're tired of all those mismatched dishes and china, invest in a new, all-white set. Good-looking, clean-lined white dinnerware is readily available at affordable prices. Keep it simple. You can't go wrong with white because you can embellish it as you set your table for various occasions.

Music that might accompany this space? Maybe something by Diana Krall for the meal, but Ella Fitzgerald for the setup. It's all about creating the right mood with music—the soundtrack to your day.

IDEAS
you can look for and use

How do you display your dishware? Could open shelves benefit you? If you have vintage china or dinnerware that has been passed down in your family, display it on the open shelves of your hutch.

Do you hide cookbooks or put them out and use them? This dining room is continuous with the kitchen and its desk area, so the cookbooks on the shelves become part of the dining room environment. Note the art propped on the desk and on the countertop in the kitchen. Adding (waterproof) art to kitchen and dining spaces makes them feel furnished rather than utilitarian.

To make dining more enjoyable, keep the view from the dining table uncluttered. A messy kitchen or countertops full of small appliances can take away from the mood you want to create.

Personality Plus

This home captures the essence of layering. Pieces brought together from travels, over time, over space, from impulse buys, to things the owners had as children—these are things that became the foundation of who they are as grownups and as homeowners. Sometimes the casual style of putting together pieces that are not a set produces some the best results.

I like this space because it is whimsical. There are lots of rich, unexpected details that individually would make the room formal, yet all together give the room a relaxed, well-lived-in feel. For example, the crystal chandelier is very ornate, something you would expect in a traditional dining room, yet in this eclectic mix it adds a layer of magic. The farmhouse windows are classic in line and distressed, while the raw linen drapery is luxurious and elegant, pulled simply to one side to billow down to the floor in a puddle.

Mismatched chairs suit the purpose of seating, yet each has a story, a history about it, as does the round table. I like round tables for meals because everyone is equal and can more easily join in the conversation.

To add to the whimsy, mini-lantern lights are draped around doorways, tea canisters hold flowers from the garden, and the dog has a seat at the table. By the way, the dog in these pictures did not pose. He got up on the chair and was ready for his close-up. I turned to look at the table and there he was. Animals are very much part of the tapestry of life.

*Arrange mini-lantern lights around a door for a whimsical look

*White paint unifies mismatched furniture

In this kind of room there should always be music playing in the background. When I present a final reveal of a room to a client, I always have music playing. Music sets a tone and becomes part of the memory of the experience. So when someone sees his or her room for the first time, the first impression is more emotional because of whatever music is playing.

I could imagine Joni Mitchell's "The Circle Game" softly playing in this room. What's your room's musical theme song? Music also helps during cleanup after the meal. Remember that scene in the film *The Big Chill* where the guests all clean up after the big dinner while "Ain't Too Proud To Beg" is playing?

A postscript on this dining room: I revisited recently, and now this dining room is a sitting room/home office. It costs nothing to change furniture around and give rooms new purpose!

*Crystal chandelier adds elegance

*Raw linen panel pulls to the side for a casual look

IDEAS
you can look for and use

String lights are a fun option and a creative budget-saver for lighting accents. They add mood and cost next to nothing.

Painted floors can truly open up a space and make a smaller room seem bigger. They also allow natural light to bounce around the room.

Try mixing chairs of different styles around a table. Painting them all the same color unifies them, but if you like more variety, you could paint them different colors. Either way, having unexpected options for seating keeps things fun.

The light fixture over the table is on a pulley system so when the table is used for dining, it can be pulled down over the table. When the room is a sitting room, it can be up above head height. Add a mini-shade to each light bulb for a whole new lighting effect in your space.

In summer, go into your yard and pick a bunch of wildflowers or leaves and put them in a pitcher, jar, or interesting glassware for your table. This is a fine example of just treating yourself to something nice.

I like round tables for meals because everyone is equal and can more easily join in the conversation.

This is the kind of house I grew up in: a very traditional, one-level, ranch-style home built in the 1960s. What is striking about it is how architecture that feels so "yesterday" can find a modern face while retaining the basics.

This is the dining room of the house shown on page 68. It would have been a small-scale living room in the old days, but now it is the everyday dining room. The old main entrance to the house is still there, but the family and visitors use a newly added sunroom/mudroom entrance off the kitchen for everyday access.

Typical of many houses across the country, this house previously had popcorn ceilings. Trendy at the time, now the treatment is a headache for homeowners who are making over their rooms. In this case, Venetian plaster saved the day and added a layer of rich style and dimension. It actually gives the illusion that the space is much larger than it is. The walls and ceiling are finished in the same material and hue with no crown molding, blending them enough to create the feeling of more height and space. This wall finish also tends to bounce light off the surface, which increases the sense of airy openness. Welcome to the modern ranch-style house.

The soundtrack here for a Sunday brunch might be something by Debussy to even Nora Jones or Natalie Merchant.

IDEAS
you can look for and use

See how the table almost looks like an old drafting table? Sometimes unexpected things can make for interesting table options. You might fine great barn wood for a top and a set of vintage wrought-iron legs for the base. I've even seen large metal garden urns used as a base with a big piece of glass as a top. Be creative.

The spark of color in the chairs adds a new hue and warmth to the room. Pieces of furniture like this can help introduce favorite colors into your space.

A sideboard or buffet can be used in a dining room for storing food and wine as well as table linens, and the top gives you a surface for display. Instead of the usual china hutch or buffet, what about using a dresser? Furniture in the dining room doesn't always have to be "dining room furniture."

Notice the frames around the artwork. Gold frames catch the light and add some sparkle to the room, and using gold on all three unifies them.

Trim work such as door frames and baseboards is typically slender and functional in ranch houses. Here, the homeowners painted the trim to accent the walls. You can add trim to a room to give it traditional character or take it away for a more streamlined look. What works best for your home?

Note the lighting. Instead of a chandelier or pendant over the dining table, the room has recessed ceiling lights. This gives the room more flexibility—it doesn't always have to be a dining room.

*Recessed lights instead of a chandelier allow flexibility in furniture arrangement and room function

*Venetian plaster on walls and ceilings adds depth and richness

Farmhouse-Fresh

My camera couldn't stop clicking when I went to shoot this family home. It had an air of artistic style with the works of art, the seating choices, the long table, and the sunny faces of the children, not to mention the perfect summer day outside. It's the kind of setting where you can imagine the smell of brewing coffee, with an undercurrent of burnt firewood from last winter's fires in the potbelly stove nearby.

Old houses have pipes in strange places, but you don't have to hide them—just paint them to match the walls.

One item to note is the beadboard wainscot. One of my favorite combos is white beadboard wainscot in a room with butter-yellow walls. Butter yellow says a sunny day to me, but you could also use red, sage green, or robin's-egg blue. The height of the wainscot in this room is typical (about chair-back height), but I also like to extend it up to about 5 feet whether the ceiling is low or high. The separation of the wood detail and the painted wall above adds great depth to a room. In a small room with high wainscoting, painting the upper part of the walls and the ceiling the same color makes the room feel larger because you don't notice as much where the walls end and the ceiling starts.

The music for this space would be a soft piano sound, maybe something from George Winston's album *December*, or to liven it up, maybe Sarah McLachlan, a big-band sound with Harry Connick, Jr., or the soundtrack from *When Harry Met Sally*.

*Beadboard wainscoting defines country style

*Different flooring defines different zones—wood for dining, tile for the kitchen

IDEAS
you can look for and use

Artwork can really add color and style to any room. Know any artists whose work you love?

The straight, simple lines of the table, bench, and end chairs make a statement that's almost modern—farmhouse style for a new century.

Old houses have pipes in strange places, but you don't have to hide them—just paint them to match the walls. To me, that's part of what gives an old house so much character.

Floors that are original to a house should be saved and enjoyed. Sometimes a simple buffing or waxing does the trick. Old floors that show wear have a history, and you should work with it and not lose that.

*One large painting gives the room a focus

Collected with Love

This dining room spoke to me about the love of collecting. You know when you see a piece of furniture and you just fall in love with it? Sometimes you make decisions with your heart regardless of what's practical for your life now. I could imagine finding a table like the one on the next page, feeling I had to have it even though I had no place for it, and buying and storing it. In fact, I've done that before. Eventually, the right space comes along. It finds its way home, if you will.

The same applies to objects. One day you find yourself collecting old dish ware or candlesticks. Before you know it, you have lots of them. In this home, brown creamware pitchers and serving dishes were the collection that came into focus over time, eventually finding a beautiful home in this young family's dining room.

When you buy vintage furniture or antiques, you're making their history part of your history. As you collect, think about what you will be leaving behind for others to enjoy after you're gone. Make choices that speak to you now, and your good taste will resonate for years to come. It's nice to think that someday this baby will surround herself with things that her mother had once loved. What are your own children going to cherish that you loved so much? What will they look at decades from now and know that it gave you much happiness?

The background music choice here would be the CD *Summer* by the artist of the same name.

*Use a dining room hutch to show off a special collection

IDEAS
you can look for and use

Collections have more impact if you display them as a group. See how this homeowner has arranged like pieces together in orderly groups? Only on the top shelf does she alternates tall and short teapots, sugar bowls, and milk pitchers. The effect is clean, not cluttered. How do you display your favorite things? Could you apply this approach to your collections?

This is the kind of dining table that will stay with this family. What kind of furniture do you have? Is it heirloom quality? If not, can you upgrade to something that can stay in the family and be passed on?

Do you have inherited pieces that you value, but they don't quite make sense in your home? Try using them throughout the house. Keep the table in the dining room, but maybe use the chairs in the breakfast area and the buffet in the foyer. This is a good solution if the pieces are more formal than your own taste, yet you want to make them work in your home.

For a quick change in the dining room, buy ready-made slipcovers to drape over the chairs. The fabric gives the whole room a new look and lets you to have some fun with your key pieces.

No artwork? Think about hanging plates on plate hangers in groupings on your walls.

*Mix new chairs with a vintage table for a fresh look

The Warmth of Wood

The wood tones of this dining room make it a warm and inviting space to enter. Notice how the rich woods echo throughout the house, from the furniture, wood floors, and wide-plank walls in the dining room to the wooden doors, floors, furniture, and bookcases beyond. This unifies the spaces. If your dining room is open to other rooms like this, look for furniture that brings a common accent color into each connecting area. The wood tone in your kitchen cabinets could match the table in your dining area, for example, and also the armoire in your family room.

There are two things I love about this room that can be useful tricks for any homeowner: interior French doors between rooms and wood siding on the walls. French doors let light flow into the room, yet allow you to close off the space. They communicate that there is another room beyond that is inviting you in. This enhances the sense of space, even when the room is only a pantry or closet. If you want to hide the contents of the closet, install fabric on tension rods on the back of the door. The wood planks on a small section of wall make the room more interesting. Sometimes the unexpected can give a room more character.

Sometimes the unexpected can give a room more character.

You can add details like these by using salvaged barn wood, French doors, or even old windows. Architectural salvage is one of my favorite things. Most towns have architectural salvage shops that sell great pieces saved from old houses. Old windows can be used in interior spaces as part of a room divider wall or added to a small, dark space to provide access to natural light—maybe a hallway, half-bath, or between kids' rooms. You can insert etched or frosted-glass panes for privacy while still allowing light to shine through. The soundtrack for this space might be something by Andrea Bocelli.

*Similar wood tones connect adjoining rooms

*Use salvaged barn wood to add warmth and richness

IDEAS
you can look for and use

The mixing of wood tones works well here. The flooring, wall, and most furniture pieces are in the same medium-brown range with a red undertone, while the dining chairs are painted black. It's okay to mix woods—it adds richness.

Using French doors for interior doors separates the rooms but still allows light to flow in.

Fresh flowers are a treat, but plants and greenery save money over time and add a vibrancy to the space. Plus, some plants act as an air purifier in your room.

*Chandelier and rug placement help set the dining area apart

Formal Dining

This dining room is more formal and traditional, but still comfortable. Substantial upholstered chairs surround an expandable wood table with a matching sideboard. The neutral tones of the walls are classic and clean. The window (visible in the mirror) is bare to enhance the richness, you could easily add velvet drapery panels to the windows. Windows don't always need to be covered up, but in winter, draperies would enclose the room and make it more romantic. That brings up the question of drapery length. I like the panels to be long enough to bunch or puddle on the floor, but if you don't want to bother with adjusting the extra fabric, have the hems just skim the floor. Keep it easy for yourself.

This room is flexible enough for a seated Thanksgiving meal or a serve-yourself buffet—just pull the chairs away and set out food and drinks on the table and the sideboard.

The oversized mirror bounces light around and gives the illusion of more space, a useful trick for smaller dining rooms as well as large ones. The seasonal wheat display on the buffet could be replaced with two tall table lamps for added warmth.

One other thought about this room: The straight, clean lines of the table and buffet are based on historical European styles but the chairs are transitional, so it would be easy to tip this room toward a more modern look. Just replace the existing light fixture with a single oversized drum-shade pendant, add a modern area rug, and you have an instant update.

Music here . . . one my favorites when I'm cooking a meal and setting the table is singer Madeleine Peyroux. She's like a modern-day Billie Holiday.

IDEAS
you can look for and use

If you like a traditional style but you don't want to be completely formal, think about having a modern drum shade over the table instead of a more traditional light fixture. Or instead of having a mirror over the buffet, hang a large modern painting or a group of black-and-white photos.

The formal setting and large table allow you to make the table the center of attention when you entertain. Make the most of it with great-looking dish ware, glassware, placemats, votives, napkins, and a centerpiece to add color, a theme, or a mood. A quick centerpiece: Lay a long, frameless mirror (the kind installed in closets) on the table, add pillar candles of various heights, mix in some cut greenery from shrubbery in your yard, and scatter some clementine oranges—instant style.

*Oversized mirror enhances the illusion of space

*Clean-lined upholstered chairs are transitional between contemporary and modern

Everyday Dining

Clean and simple are the words that come to mind with this room. It's the kind of room that can easily be used for everyday dining. The table and chairs have an almost Southwestern feeling about them, yet can work in a traditional family setting in a suburban house. The red accents make it more festive and uplifting. The Roman shades don't hide the window moldings but provide privacy and light control when needed. They also infuse color into the space, which is carried through to the seat cushions and could be carried to the dinnerware as well. You can see how easy it would be to give this room a new personality with new seat cushions, new lampshades or a new fixture, new window treatments, and an area rug. With good basics, style changes can happen almost instantly.

A great centerpiece idea for this table: a wooden tray, some nice-looking jars or glassware for brushes and pens/pencils, and instead of placemats, a sketchbook for each member of the family. Sit down for dinner and during dessert have everyone draw something—even the nonartists! Have a weekly family art show.

A soothing favorite for a meal here would be any of the CDs by my favorite duo Secret Garden. Their music is very cinematic and visual with the use of violin. In fact, their music is what I usually have playing in my work studio as I'm designing. It's very uplifting and evocative.

IDEAS
you can look for and use

Notice the shades. You don't have to have drapes in a dining room. Roman shades can give you privacy, control light, and bring in color.

Because of all the natural light here, the walls could easily be painted the deep red found in the shades and the room would still work. If you are thinking about adding more color in your home, the dining room is a good place to try it because lighting will be a big part of the presentation (or it should be).

*Roman shades don't hide window trim

*Change cushions for a new look

Dining in Color

The dining room is a good place to experiment with bold color on the walls, particularly a warm color such as burnt orange, red, or cocoa brown. Lit by candlelight or lamplight, it's warm and romantic and creates an inviting environment for conversation and enjoying food. By daylight, it is dynamic and exciting and makes a great backdrop for wood furnishings. Strong wall color works especially well with white or cream-color woodwork—the light trim gives the eye a place to rest and keeps the bolder hue from feeling overwhelming. In the dining room below, white woodwork contrasts with warm walls, and red lampshades, rug, and seat cushions pull out the red undertones in the wall color. Black chairs and accessories accent the color scheme.

If you're not sure you want to wrap the room in color, choose a neutral for the walls and add color at the windows, on the chair cushions, and in the accessories. The room on the previous page is a good example of using strong color sparingly to brighten a neutral space.

The dining room should reflect your tastes and the way you live. Don't be afraid to mix it up a bit.

IDEAS
you can look for and use

Give the dining room a new personality with new seat cushions, new lampshades on the chandelier, a different rug, and perhaps a table runner or tablecloth. Bare wood is beautiful, but if you get tired of too much brown, a colorful cloth can give some relief.

Shades or draperies? Shades are tailored and unfussy, but floor-to-ceiling panels soften large windows and create a more formal feeling. Draperies are also a nice way to bring in some pattern and to accent the main color scheme.

Open-Plan Ideas

What if your problem isn't that you have a separate dining room that's underused, but rather, you want a dining room and don't have one? Carving out a special space for dining in an open-plan house is easy—set up the table, surround it with chairs, and that space instantly says, "Dine here."

If your dining room is in the traffic path from the living area to the outdoors, define it as a separate space with a large area rug (below). A console table and a pair of lamps help anchor the floating dining space to one wall. To tie it visually to the surrounding spaces, you might repeat wood tones, with a table in the dining area that has the same tone as the coffee table or console table in the living space nearby.

Half-walls with columns help separate a dining area from the adjacent kitchen and living spaces in an open-plan house. A wood-plank ceiling and a chandelier centered over the dining table also help give the area its own identity (on the next page below).

In a U-shaped floor plan (on the next page above), where the kitchen, breakfast area, and dining area are separate but open to each other, unify the spaces with color. A wall color in the dining room can be introduced as an accent color in the kitchen around the corner.

Whatever your dining room's style and mood, remember that you control the environment. Set the table, add details, bring in good food, and always create a mood—dim lights, candles, and music help set the stage. Be good to yourself and your family.

*Console table behind sofa helps separate living area from dining area

*Area rug under the table defines eating area as its own space

*Corner fireplace shared by dining room and breakfast area

*In this open-floor plan, the half-wall separates the living and dining spaces

CREATIVE
thoughts

Some more food for thought . . .

1 A three-season porch is perfect for warm-weather dining and relaxing. In addition to the usual wicker furniture, consider bringing a secondhand table and vintage chairs out for a truly furnished feeling.

2 Instead of paintings or photos, try stringing rope or twine and small lights across the wall. Use clothespins to suspend your kids' artwork—instant art wall! At night it all adds a warm glow to the dining experience.

3 Fun wall décor gives your dining room personality. A folk-art flag painted on wood, old advertising signs, or an antique quilt can make an interesting alternative to traditional art.

4 Vintage china can have great detail and color. Use that as part of the inspiration for your space if you are not sure what color to go with.

5 For an instant casual visual, fill mason jars with everyday utensils on your sideboard or hutch for easy access. Use what you have in creative ways.

6 Dining rooms can be dual-purpose rooms for reading, playing games, or hosting your book club. Pull the chairs away from the table and you start to see new possibilities.

7 It's okay to mix upholstered chairs with wood chairs in your dining room. Add a bench to the mix for casual seating that can always hold one more.

8 Red is popular for dining rooms, but the right shade is key. Try a sample patch of paint on the wall and see it at various times of day, especially times when you might entertain most. Evening light is very different from bright sunlight. That affects the color and mood.

9 Use outdoor dining chairs inside. French folding bistro chairs can be a budget-friendly way to make your room come to life.

10 Flowers complete a room. They show that you took some time on the details to make it special. Whether it's a bunch from your garden or a bouquet from the corner market, treat yourself and your guests.

11 A crisp linen tablecloth makes a beautiful base. Build the table from there. For a budget-friendly alternative, invest in an inexpensive flat sheet in your favorite color and use that.

12 Think about what you need to have on hand as you entertain: wine, glasses, bottles of water, candles, linens. This will help guide you as you decide how much storage you need.

HOW
to begin?

Here are some questions to ask yourself as you consider ways to make your dining room look and function better.

How often do you use your dining room?

How else could you use your current dining space? Could your dining room be a library, too? A craft room? A home office?

Could the closet in your dining room be transformed into a craft/art closet for the kids to use with their friends, using the covered dining table for their creations?

Could that same closet be turned into a home office nook? Open the doors and you have your fax, printer, and office equipment, and the dining table is your daytime desk. When it's time for dinner, just close the doors.

What about positioning your dining table in a new way instead of centering it in the room? A pendant light doesn't always have to be the focal point of the dining room.

Could you have a built-in bench in a corner and place your table there with chairs around the open sides for a less formal feeling? That might free up space for a seating area with chairs and maybe a loveseat. The room could become a great place for playing games and talking about your day.

As you look at furniture, what style are you going for? Do you like fabric-covered chairs or all wood? Do you like to mix it up—a bench on one side with chairs on the other? Go online and type in "dining room images" in your search engine. What images do you respond to?

Do you like a farmhouse table or do you prefer a more formal style with ornate legs? Maybe you have had a rectangular table and now the time has come for a round table?

What about flooring? Wood floor? Carpet? Tile? If you have pets and kids, easy cleanup is key.

Your dining room is a chance to create a moodier room, so what wall colors would you like? What colors do you know you *don't* want? What would be your dream color?

How do you see yourself entertaining in this space? If it is a larger space, do you want to have room for lots of people seated at your table? If it is a smaller space, could you have casual buffet dinners that allow people to move around without sitting at the table? Make your space work for you. If you are not formal as a person, don't make the dining room formal. If you like it casual, keep it casual. There are no rules as to what is right or wrong.

How do you want to set the stage? How do you want this room to feel? One way to get at the mood you want to create is to think about your favorite restaurant. Why is going there memorable for you? What is the lighting like? Is it moody and romantic or bright and uplifting? Is the seating casual and comfortable or more formal and classic? Do you have to dress up or is it a jeans-and-tee-shirt kind of place? These details might help you bring to life the feeling you want for your own dining room. To me, half the journey of getting the right design in place is getting the right feel or mood.

Personal Sanctuary

The bedroom is where you begin and end each day. It is such an important part of daily life, yet most people put the design of the bedroom on the back burner. The rest of the house is "done" from a design standpoint, and even the kids' rooms look great, but the parents' room is left to become an afterthought or a catch-all room for miscellaneous pieces of furniture. You just close the door and say "I'll deal with that room later." "Later" becomes months, and time flies by. This room could do so much for you, but it stays stuck in time and zaps your energy level.

The bedroom should be energizing, uplifting, relaxing, soothing—whatever meets your needs in this space. It shouldn't be about someone else's idea of a bedroom, but rather, what *you* like. It's not like any other room in your house, because *you* are the one you're designing for.

You can't control what life hands you, but you *can* create a safe and inviting world inside your home. Why not make your bedroom a space you actually like being in? Even if you don't have a big budget to be creative with, there are things you can easily do to make it more comfortable and much more of a haven for yourself.

A haven. That is a good word to describe what a bedroom can or should be—a place to get away from it all and recharge. It does not matter what size bedroom you have. It's how you work what you have that counts. I think the bottom line is to surround yourself with things you love.

A bedroom should be a haven—a place to get away from it all and recharge.

Step-by-Step Makeover

Here is an example of a bedroom evolving from bland and uninviting to welcoming. The room was a wide-open white box. In "stage one," the bed with its padded headboard stood against the wall parallel to take in the view of the lake. With the birth of their first child, the couple placed the baby's bassinet in front of the windows.

After the baby moved to the nursery, the parents upgraded to a new iron headboard, which they placed in front of the windows. They no longer woke up to a view of the lake, but the new arrangement combined the room's two focal points, the view and the bed.

Step 1: Clear Out the Space

To bring this room to life—to make it a truly comfortable haven—we began by taking out the main pieces so we could clearly see the room overall. Then we could play around with the placement of the main pieces. To figure out where the room's focal point is, I stand in the entrance to the room and see where my gaze falls. What do I see first? In this room, the view of the lake through the windows was obviously important, but at night the bed is the focal point rather than the outdoors. So returning the bed to the wall where they had it originally allowed the homeowners to enjoy the lake view in the morning but put the focus on the bed at night.

Step 2: Add Color

The next phase of bringing this bedroom to life was to add color. Using the natural world outside as inspiration, I chose a sage green for the walls to pick up on the evergreens and the hues of the lake. Inspiration for wall color can come from bed linens, a chair fabric, or a work of art. This is when your Look Book comes in handy.

Step 3: Arrange Furniture

As soon as the room was painted, the mood began to shift. Next came reusing what they had that was worth keeping—a dresser, a nightstand, and a console table near the bed. We reshuffled these pieces to see what worked best where. A dresser now doubles as a nightstand, and a chair that wasn't needed in the family room came in to create a reading nook by the windows, along with the existing console table.

Step 4: Add Softness

Bedrooms are all about comfort, so the next layer for this space was softness. This is usually achieved with bedding and window treatments. Because there are so many windows in this room, it was important to use window treatments to control light and privacy while framing the view.

BEFORE

Matchstick shades take care of the first requirement and lush drapery panels handle the second. You may not want to cover your windows, but keep in mind that treatments on windows can make a room cozier and more inviting. They can also hide a not-so-great view or outdated, uninteresting windows. Window treatments can make a boring window seem much more impressive and substantial.

Bedding should be the best quality you can afford. At a minimum, look for high-thread-count sheets. A featherbed pad on your mattress, a good set of sheets, and a down

Bedroom colors are not set in stone in terms of what is "right." The right color is truly what you like.

BEFORE

*Dog picture inspired accessory colors

*A dresser doubles as a nightstand

comforter to top it off can make you feel like you're waking up in a Paris hotel. Add several goose-down pillows to make it perfect (unless you are allergic to feathers, in which case look for hypoallergenic fillings that are just as soft as down). Spread a folded duvet or blanket at the end of the bed, and the layered, turned-down-bed look will convince you that you're walking into a magazine spread each day.

Step 5: Details

The final layer of the bedroom is the detail—the personal touches that make it come to life. In this room, a dog painting with vivid cranberry tones suggested the accent color for the area rug, the table lampshades, the accessories, and the flowers. That painting also inspired bringing in more art to cover a once-blank wall. If you love art, bring more in.

The lamps offer another fun way to personalize the room. The red shades stay in place year-round, but the glass bases can be filled with different items according to the season. For the holidays, we poured in some sand from the lake shore, added Christmas balls and greenery, and tucked in a vintage post card.

*Chair and console create a reading nook

IDEAS
you can look for and use

Once you have determined the focal point of your bedroom, bring the things you like back into the space. In most cases, you do not have to go out and buy all new stuff.

If you don't have a headboard, try living without one for awhile and use big Euro pillows against the wall to create a headboard effect.

If you have a larger room, create a seating area using extra furniture from your living room.

If you have small or narrow windows, simply extending the curtain rod a few feet beyond each side of the window frame can give an insignificant window more visual weight.

Is there a piece of artwork you could use to inspire colors for accessories?

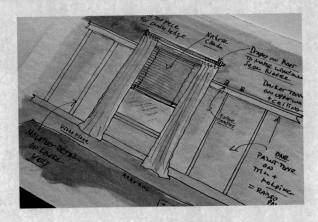

Modern Living

When I walked into this room I felt transported to a luxury hotel in Miami even though the cold winds of a New England winter were blowing outside. The Delano Hotel in Miami is famous for its white-on-white interiors. The use of white and cream in room details gives a sense of luxury and style, and evokes a calm, serene atmosphere. At the same time, the white-on-white scheme allows the view framed by the wonderful windows to take center stage. Imagine winter snows making the room even brighter on sunny days; or in spring and summer, the lush green of trees and grass emphasizing the cooling effect of the pale scheme.

This room obviously has plenty of space for a sleeping area, a desk, a TV, and a generous sitting area. You may not have room for a king-size bed or a separate sitting area, but you can still bring this calming mood to life in your own room. Choose shades of cream, ivory, and white for walls, trim, furniture, carpeting, and accessories. Notice that the furniture is clean-lined and contemporary, and there are not a lot of accessories cluttering the surfaces.

*A variety of textures and tone-on-tone pattern add interest to a one-color room

IDEAS
you can look for and use

A neutral color scheme has a calming effect, but to keep it from being boring, use a variety of textures, from satiny-smooth to rougher textures, to add depth.

To create this kind of serene mood in your bedroom, keep furnishings simple and get rid of visual clutter.

Gather simple collections of matching items (such as the vases on the table) to create a focal point on a table or dresser.

If you don't have space for a sitting area, perhaps a corner with a comfortable chair can become your reading nook.

Window treatments can give you privacy but they can also control the levels of light. If you have a lot of windows, you might want to install curtains or shades to filter strong sunlight. If you have a spectacular view, keep the treatments simple.

Seen a hotel suite that you loved? Maybe you can re-create that look in your own bedroom.

*This contemporary
bed has clean lines

*The end table isn't cluttered
with a lot of accessories

Peaceful Traditional

This bedroom creates a peaceful feeling with its classic cottage style. In contrast to the modern white bedroom, this room is furnished with black-painted pieces that reproduce antique furnishings. So you can still have the soothing color palette on the walls and lots of white to convey a calming mood, but anchor the look with contrasting color on key pieces of furniture. Black adds visual drama, especially when it's repeated in accessories such as lamps, mirrors, and even framed artwork. Layer on softness with bedding, a slipper chair and ottoman slipcovered in white, and an area rug.

Imagine this room with floral wallpaper, a quilt on the bed, and maybe different bedside lamps, and you can see that what is now clean and crisp could easily become country. Using accessories to change your style direction is much more affordable than buying new furniture when your tastes change.

Black adds visual drama, especially when it's repeated in accessories.

*A slip-covered bench for additional seating would be perfect here

*Bedding with pattern could bring in seasonal change

*Matching bedside tables and lamps create symmetrical balance for a calm, stable mood.

*A box-pleated skirt adds tailored flair to slipcovers

IDEAS
you can look for and use

Look at the main furniture pieces in your room and decide what kind of scene you want to set. Furniture with classic lines can look modern or country, depending on what you surround it with.

Use black to anchor a room visually. Balance it with lots of white or lighter colors so the effect is dramatic rather than dark.

If you like all-white bedding but still want to add color, introduce tone on the walls with paint and carry a small amount of that color through into fabrics, such as pillows or a duvet cover.

Slipcovers are great because they are washable. With slipcovers, you can live with white, even in a house with kids and pets. Just make sure the fabric is machine washable (which I like) or can be dry-cleaned.

If this room had draperies on the windows, you could also introduce a drapery rod and panels behind the bed. This would create a frame for the bed area that would draw the eye even more as you enter the room. The other advantage of draperies or fabric in the room is that if you have hardwood floors, the fabric helps absorb sound.

Only have the budget for one chair in your bedroom seating area for now? You can always build upon what you have over time. Start with one and see how much you use it. Then decide whether you want a chair for the other side of the bed.

Feeling Blue

Color on bedroom walls can make the room's mood go in one direction or another. This is why I suggest people test out a paint color in a small area first and watch how the color changes in daylight and by lamplight. You may not spend your whole day in your bedroom, but you want to like going in there. Bedroom colors are not set in stone in terms of what is "right." The right color is truly what *you* like: Darker colors can create a warm, rich environment, while light and airy colors can evoke a serene, at-peace mood.

The blue on these walls has just a hint of green in it, which makes it a warm blue. With the warm wood tones of the floors and furniture, the room feels restful but not chilly—a danger with certain shades of pure blue. Notice that bedding, accessories, and accents bring in blues and blue-greens that are darker and lighter than the walls. Using a range of tones keeps the color scheme interesting.

Although this room is not large, the owners made space for a reading corner by bringing in a smaller-scale chaise. Bare wood floors add richness to the room. Wall-to-wall carpeting would give it an entirely different feel. Whether you choose wood floors or carpet for your bedroom is purely personal preference. Wood floors add to the value of your home, and you can use area rugs to soften the room and protect high-traffic areas. Wall-to-wall carpeting is warmer on your feet on cold mornings and it helps muffle sound. To me, the deciding factor is maintenance. What will be easier for you to take care of? If you have kids and pets running around, carpeting traps dust and hair and can be damaged by spills, but it's soft on little feet and knees. Think about how you live and what is most important to you in terms of everyday care as you research products and finishes.

*Bedding colors play off the wall hue

*A fabric panel pulled to one side helps soften the window

*Shades that fit snugly inside the window frame let the trimwork show

Painting

I hate painting walls—it's boring. When I did television makeovers of homes, part of the project was to paint the rooms on camera. I would open the can of paint, dip in the brush, and show the color going up on the walls. The viewers and the homeowner could instantly see how color would change the room and make it come to life. Paint makes change happen instantly and gives you control over the result.

The feeling of accomplishment that comes from painting a room yourself is motivating. My wife and I recently painted a room in our house. I was dreading it, but working together, we finished in a weekend, and the results were very gratifying. The essence of the room changed. I may not enjoy the process of painting, but what it gives me in the end is far greater than the process. Of course, if you have high ceilings, intricate moldings, and details, it may be much more gratifying to hire a professional!

IDEAS
you can look for and use

Use color to create the atmosphere you want in the bedroom. Test paint colors in a small area first to see how light affects them.

Consider maintenance when you choose your bedroom flooring—what will be easiest for you to keep clean and looking good?

Can you create a reading corner by bringing in a small chair and a lamp?

The drapery panel at the window adds a softening fabric accent to the room. That same type of panel could be used for a closet-door makeover. Remove your bulky closet door, install a curtain rod over it, and add some fabric panels. Sometimes removing doors can save space. Plus, the fabric can bring in color, texture, and pattern and makes a nice alternative to doors.

If you have great moldings around your windows, shutters allow you to have privacy and light control without covering up the trim work. With white window frames, you would probably want white shutters; with stained trim, choose stained shutters.

CREATIVE
thoughts

Here are some more ways to make your bedroom a haven.

1 Don't forget final touches like candles, incense, or flowers to finish off the bedroom.

2 Fill bowls or baskets with things you love from your travels or favorite keepsakes to make your space personal.

3 Enjoy being in your bed. This is where I say splurge a bit on nice sheets or comforters.

4 In the old days, slipcovers were changed seasonally—lighter fabrics in summer and darker, patterned ones for winter months. Now it is all about ease of use. Just throw them in the wash when they need freshening. To me, they get better with each wash.

5 Using various sizes of pillows can make a bed more visually appealing. You don't have to go overboard, but layers of Euro, standard, and throw-size pillows mixed together make the bed a focal point and create an inviting look. Top the bed with a down comforter and a duvet, and you've got covers that keep you warm at night and make the bed—literally.

6 Be inventive with headboard options. Use doors, either antique or new, to add architectural interest behind the bed. Mount them to the wall, add crown molding on top, and you have an instant headboard.

7 Although your dog may end up on your bed, don't forget to give him a bed, too!

8 If you have family heirlooms or old pieces you love, find ways to introduce them in the room and bring them to life in a new space.

9 Accessories offer simple ways to bring in style or a theme. Smaller props add a final layer but do not need to break the bank. This is a place to have some fun.

10 Create a corner with a chair and ottoman or a chaise—just a place to hang out for yourself.

11 Bedrooms can be very clean and simple. They do not have to be overstuffed with accessories and busy to the eye.

12 Family photos and art are a must-have in any room, but especially in the bedroom. Black-and-white images stand out even more when surrounded by the colors in this corner.

HOW
to begin?

As you get ready to decorate or make over your bedroom, ask yourself these questions. Write down your answers to help you with your planning.

What size bed do you need? Is a queen size big enough? Would a king-size bed overpower the room? Sometimes beds can be too big for a room. Think about what you need and also the positioning of the bed in your room.

Do you need a headboard? If so, do you want something new or something vintage? Could you build one or be creative with draping instead of using a typical headboard? Buying a new headboard is an investment and will be in the room for a while. Make choices that can stand the test of time instead of opting for what is trendy right now.

Do you need nightstands on either side of the bed? What do you want the nightstands to do? Store stuff? Display stuff? Give you lots of room for a reading lamp, books, an alarm clock, flowers, and so on by your side? Do you prefer matching or mismatched pieces? It's a very personal space, so make it your own.

Do you need a dresser or do your closets have plenty of storage? If you are a couple, do you need one dresser for each of you? Maybe you'd like cubbies with wicker baskets for storage instead of dressers. Maybe you

prefer an old-fashioned armoire for clothing storage. Can you use under-the-bed storage? How much stuff do you need to store in your bedroom? Bedroom storage comes in all shapes and sizes; assess what you have to store and decide what you want out of sight and what you want to display. Check your Look Book for creative storage solutions.

Do you have space for another area in your bedroom aside from the bed area—a reading/sitting area, a desk, a workout area, a yoga area, a place to watch TV? Determine what other pieces of furniture you might need in your space and plan the room accordingly.

As you look at catalogs or browse home stores, what linens or bedding appeals to you? Are there colors you could use in the room? Do you like patterns, florals, stripes, or solids? Do you like mixing styles or do you like all-white bedding?

Do you need window treatments? Do you want privacy or the ability to control light? Do you like to sleep in complete darkness or do you like to see the moon at night?

What is the flooring? Are you dealing with wall-to-wall carpet, hardwood, or tile? Could changing the flooring change the feel of your room? Area rugs soften a room and can also add a more interesting visual layer over boring wall-to-wall carpets. Think about how the flooring might feel under your feet as you get out of bed in the morning.

Is there enough light in your room? Would bedside lamps be enough, or do you need other lighting such as floor lamps, sconces, or overhead lights? What tasks might you need lighting for? Do you like being able to control the levels of light? Would dimmers serve you well in the bedroom?

chapter 9

Working from Home

Whether you work from home or just need an area for paying the bills and checking e-mails, a home office is an opportunity. It's a chance to create a space that you love to be in because it's laid out in a way that works well for you and surrounds you with things you enjoy.

What kind of home office do you need? If you are meeting with clients and conducting virtual conferences, you'll want a separate room with a private entrance and furnishings that create a professional environment. If your at-home work is solitary, you may be able to get by with a dual-purpose guest room or dining room or even an armoire office. If your home office is mostly for paying bills, shopping online, and checking e-mails, a desk in a corner of the kitchen may be all that's required.

There is nothing like an organized, efficient, functional, and visually appealing work space to invigorate you and motivate you to stay focused.

Designating a room as a home office gives you a place to gather your work, your bills, your creative projects, and so on and know that when you are in there, it's time to focus on the tasks at hand. When work time is over, you can close the door on it. Even if you can't set aside one room for an office, it can be helpful to give yourself a way to close up shop when you're finished for the day. In one of the first places my wife and I lived, we converted a double closet in a hallway for our home office. Behind the double doors, we had a desk surface set on two file cabinets with space for a chair in between. Open shelving above the desk held books, storage baskets of files, and things we liked looking at. On the wall we hung a collage of photos, sketches, favorite quotes, etc.—things that were pleasing—for us to enjoy as we worked. When the doors were open, we could focus on work. When we closed the doors, we could leave the work mode behind. I think being able to separate work and home time is good, whether your office is a setup like that closet, an armoire office, or a separate room.

Over the years, my home office areas have ranged from that hallway closet to an armoire in my living room, an enclosed porch area, and a whole room that now serves as my creative space. I have always viewed my home office as a place I should enjoy going to every day. So aside from having the basics—phone, computer, printer/scanner, CD player—I have surrounded myself with things that I love. Family photos, my kids' art, my own artwork, books that I enjoy, a favorite incense (piñon incense from the Southwest is my favorite), and attractive notebooks and file folders make the work process more enjoyable.

Any home office space, whether it's a separate room or a corner of the kitchen, needs to be organized. I have learned over the years that the busier or more stressed I get, the more I need to stay organized. My mind is churning with ideas most of the time, so I don't need a messy desk or visuals around me that will clutter that up or get in the way of my work.

I do allow myself one area to be a bit messy, although it is a layered, thought-out messiness. I have a wall in my office that is my "vision board." It's simply a tapestry of images, tear sheets, postcards, notes, words of wisdom, and other visual things that inspire me or make me smile. I have layered these things on the wall with tacky gum that doesn't ruin the paint or put holes in the wall, and over time it has become like a piece of art. Try this in your own home office—gather things you love, images of things you are striving for or dreaming about, and create something that empowers and inspires you. Change it around from time to time to keep your vision fresh and new.

Whether you work from home or simply need a place to manage household business, remember you are at home. You are in control of this work environment, so why not enjoy the space? In the end, there is nothing like an organized, efficient, functional, and visually appealing work space to invigorate you and motivate you to stay focused.

The home offices that follow offer ideas for those who have just a small area to work in as well as for those who have a whole room. These examples may even help you discover bonus space that you have never thought of as having office potential—the attic, the basement, or an extra closet. It's all in how you see it.

Attic Office

I designed this home office for a client who wanted to transform an unused attic space into a creative office space. Not being constantly reminded of work was a key goal here. Working from home can be difficult for some people because seeing piles of work waiting or flashing message lights on the answering machine makes them feel like they can never get away from the job. This is one reason why I don't recommend having your home office area in your bedroom—you don't want to wake up every day and see work stuff. You want to be able to separate yourself and designate time to it as needed in another area. So for these homeowners the space in the attic presented a fun and useful solution, finishing a space that was already roughed in.

This project required adding framing, insulation, drywall, flooring, a dormer, and windows (see Chapter 4, "Redesign or Renovate?"). In your own home, if you already have the basics in place, you are that much further ahead. Even if you have to renovate, converting unfinished space can be a good investment, adding to the value of your home when you're ready to sell. You are utilizing the existing footprint of the house, yet maximizing livable square footage. I ask people who are holding out for someday buying their dream house, what about making the home you have now better? Could your current house potentially be your dream house—if you could see it and all its areas in a new way?

With the basics in place, the next layer was creating the mood and feel of the room. I wanted it to be darker and moodier than the rest of the home, which meant dark wood furniture and a rich, warm color on the walls. Working with darker tones would be okay because this attic now had great windows for natural light, but I also planned good lighting options in the space to control levels of task and mood lighting. The home office can be a great opportunity to design a themed room. You are creating a space for yourself that you love being in, so why not have a theme or a certain style?

*Computers and a printer/copier/fax are located along one wall

*The drafting table and island allow the owners to work standing or sitting

One layer of detail that is important here is the wall finish. I chose an eco-friendly clay product to go over the drywall panels. I could certainly have painted the walls a rich color, which would have also been fine. However, I wanted to take this room to a greener level. Applying the textured clay finish to the walls not only added an instant richness and visual texture to the room, it also incorporated a product that was good for the environment. It's nontoxic and actually serves to keep the room cool in summer and warm in winter—a plus in my book.

To organize the space, I created zones: a desk area for computers, a seating area for conversation, a reading/sleeping nook, a drafting table area with a view to the outside, and the main work island in the center. It's perfect for one person to work alone, but several people could work here efficiently, too. In laying out your own office space, think about how you want to work in it. For example, in this environment, the homeowners often like to work standing up, so I included an island and drafting table. They also wanted areas to sit and be more relaxed, so I created a main seating area and the reading/sleeping nook in the corner.

A major element in any professional home office is the technology. This office has a main computer station on the desk, with room for another workstation if needed, and wireless capabilities for laptops. To save desk space, the homeowners chose a printer that can print both documents and photos as well as scan, fax, and copy. Cell phones make a home office happen anywhere. Because the couple can watch movies and their favorite TV shows on the computer via the Internet, there was no need for a separate TV.

*A sitting area for brainstorming and casual conferences

*A sleeping nook at the opposite end allows for naps

IDEAS
you can look for and use

Do you have an attic with a chimney at one end? Leaving the brick exposed gives the office a rustic feel that adds to the warmth of the space. Stone veneers could also be used to cover an old chimney. Different stone veneers give different looks, from New England fieldstone to a more Southwestern feel. If you don't have a chimney, could you create a wall accent like this using brick or stone veneers?

The windows and doors are trimmed with salvaged wood from an old barn. Left unstained and unsanded, they provide a frame for the views beyond while adding character overall. Could you add character to your office with salvaged windows or doors?

Dual work areas for the desk/computers gather the technical equipment in one area, while the center island and long drafting table by the windows allow the owners to spread out their work. How do you need to organize your space? Could you benefit from zoning areas for different tasks like this?

The daybed window seat creates a quiet zone in the office to read, sit with your laptop, or return phone calls. It's also perfect for extra houseguests. If you don't have a dormer or a nook for a window seat area like this one, think about adding a small sleeper sofa for guests to use.

Furniture is not built-in here, so desks and seating pieces can be moved around when it's time for a change. How do you like to work? Do you like the permanence of built-ins or do you prefer the flexibility of stand-alone pieces?

The layering of rustic-looking fabrics and prints instantly creates a masculine, inviting undertone to this room. Even if the walls were not textured with clay and tinted in a warm tone, the wood accents and fabrics bring that mood to life. What mood do you want your office to have? What colors, fabrics, and textures will create the kind of environment that helps you feel productive and focused?

*Multifunctional equipment saves desk space

Basement Office

The basement can be an ideal location for a home office and creative area for the family. Built-in cabinets and countertops serve as a storage wall for office supplies and a surface for the printer and computer, and provide a finished look like a kitchen. You could re-create this look easily with stock cabinets and laminate countertops. The work island in the middle of the room accommodates crafts, sewing, or other larger projects. People can sit on stools or stand. There is more storage underneath as well as in the well-stocked art closet nearby. The biggest thing that makes this room come to life is the lighting. Although it's a basement, it doesn't have an underground, cavelike feeling because it's well lit with recessed ceiling lights. The warm yellow paint on the walls also helps brighten the space.

BEFORE

*Closet for office supplies and crafting

*The work island can be used for crafts or other large projects

IDEAS
you can look for and use

Built-in cabinets and a desk provide plenty of storage and work space, and the island in the center is movable. Before you put up a wall of cabinets, however, take stock of what you want to store—boxes of paints? Bolts of fabric? Make a list of all the kinds of creative projects you're likely to be doing and think about the kinds of cabinets, shelving, and drawers that will help you store materials conveniently.

What color is best for basements? The yellow on these walls makes this windowless room seem much sunnier, but any light color can work if you have good lighting. Use under-cabinet lighting and recessed ceiling lights to eliminate shadows and provide good task illumination.

What kind of equipment do you need in your home office? Will you use a computer, printer, scanner, fax, and telephone there? To keep counterspace uncluttered, consider using an all-in-one scanner/printer/fax machine. Store out of sight the items you don't use frequently, or go wireless to minimize cables and cords.

Do you have a basement closet that you can turn into an office supply closet? I turned this storage closet into a central place for office supplies and crafting supplies. It not only looks nice when the doors are open but everything has a place in this small area. Is there an area that you can transform into an efficient creative closet? If not a closet, what about an old armoire?

Keeping an area for your digital camera to be hooked up to your computer is handy if you're in the habit of taking pictures every day. Plus, being able to print and store these photos is key. Storage boxes here provide vivid color accents to the overall design of the room and also protect the images.

*Attractive storage boxes organize and protect photos

Home Office Makeover

If there's a small extra room in your house, you have a blank slate for creating an efficient home office. For this room makeover, I took a small, boring room and made it functional and inviting.

Originally, it was a white box typical of many homes: no color on the walls, basic wall-to-wall carpet on the floor, and simple trim. These homeowners wanted to use this room every day as their working office, so it needed to be warmed up and made to feel welcoming.

The first order of business was paint and color. Instead of painting the whole room one color, I decided to have the room painted with horizontal stripes. The lighter bands are a pale sand color and the darker bands (which were taped off before painting) are a darker version of the same hue. The result actually makes the small room look larger—an optical illusion that works well, and the warm color makes the room friendly and inviting.

Next came furniture, including storage options for files and supplies, plus a corner desk for a laptop, phone, and printer. Soft tones of white and cream keep the room bright and fresh. A seating area with a chaise and table adds comfort. The lamps, which the homeowners already had, were spray-painted and given new shades. Then it was just a matter of bringing in props from around the house to pull together a look—setting the stage is always the fun part of the project!

*The horizontal stripes painted on the wall makes this small room look larger

*Matching file cabinets topped with laminate or painted plywood make a great desk

*Drawers on brackets provide display and storage

*Unfinished table gets a coat of paint

IDEAS
you can look for and use

Can simple paint effects add some character to your home office? Painting the walls with horizontal or vertical stripes in two related colors is an easy way to make the background more interesting.

Can you furnish your office using pieces from other rooms in the house? Maybe give them a new look with some spray paint? The lamps on the desk and side table were repurposed from what the homeowner already had, with a can of yellow spray paint and new shades giving them new style. Do you have similar items you can reuse?

If you don't have room for a sofa, what about a chaise? It's nice to give any home office an area for seating that is not at a desk.

BEFORE

If there's a small extra room in your house, you have a blank slate for creating an efficient home office.

Office Nooks

So what if you don't have a whole room to dedicate to a home office? Look at ways to make do with part of a room or with just a table in the corner of your living room. An office may not have to include a computer or other equipment; it could simply be a spot for writing letters (people still do that!), painting, or paying bills.

A table with leaves that fold up or down to make it smaller or larger as needed can serve as a desk in a corner of the room. There's space for a laptop and doing paperwork, but it looks nice because personal things are gathered and displayed. A table lamp illuminates the surface by night, and during the day natural light through the French doors provides light for working. Furniture that's easy to move lets you take advantage of nooks and crannies for office space. In this case, in winter the desk can be positioned in front of the French doors, but in summer the table can be repositioned to allow the doors to open. Then the terrace becomes an extension of this homeowner's office area.

A simple home office can be tucked into nearly any corner. With a laptop, lighting, and a good chair, you're ready to go.

A guest room can easily share space with a home office. By thinking about the room in a new way, the homeowner makes what could be an underused space a hardworking room that serves more than one purpose: It's a home office by day, with all of the office equipment tucked into an armoire. When the desk armoire is closed up, the room becomes a sitting area. With a loveseat that pulls out to a twin-size sleeper, the room can also serve as an instant guest room.

*A gateleg table, an armchair, and a lamp turn this corner into a workspace

*A farm table offers lots of space to spread out paperwork

An office could simply be a spot for writing letters (people still do that!).

*Tuck an office into an armoire

*A chair-and-a-half folds out to a twin bed for guests

CREATIVE
thoughts

Just some fun things to think about in your own home office . . .

1 If you have the space, set aside a room for being creative. If you don't have a whole room to spare, carve out a corner for creative activities for yourself or your family.

2 Instead of the usual desk, use metal sawhorse bases for legs (get them at the hardware store) and top them with an inexpensive surface like this brushed-metal top. Or lay a solid flat door on the sawhorses for a work surface. This kind of desk is budget-friendly and can easily be put up when you need it and taken down when you don't. This could be set up in any room of your home.

3 Gather your favorite books around you for inspiration, visual support, and reminders of things you like. Stack them on your desk or table surface. Change them around often to keep things fresh.

4 Use stones as paperweights. When the windows are open, this will keep papers from flying around. Gather favorite stones from your vacation or from your morning walk in the woods.

5 Think about supplies you need to have around you. If you paint, have your brushes and paints out and ready. If you write, have plenty of white paper and ink cartridges for your printer. Get yourself ready to be brilliant when the mood strikes.

6 Family photos personalize your space. Frame some and tack some up on a bulletin board or vision board. Print those digital photos and display to enjoy them.

7 At the market, buy a bunch of flowers of the season to put on your desk.

8 Creative repurposing brings personality to your office. An old truck holds sticky notepads.

9 Think about how much storage you need. Drawers, baskets, or nice-looking boxes can store things out of sight but still allow them to be close by. You don't always have to have file cabinets.

10 Create simple tabletop displays in your office with props and accessories. Changing them around gives you new visuals to look at every week or month. Leaning photos against the wall instead of hanging them lets you move them easily.

11 Vision boards are key to inspiring creativity and helping you focus on meeting your goals. Your Look Book can help you here too, with ideas for desks, storage, work surfaces, and more.

HOW *to begin?*

Ask yourself these questions as you consider ways to create a home office space:

Do you have a room that could be your home office?

Why doesn't the home office you have already work for you? Is it cluttered and filled with mismatched furniture? Does it feel like an afterthought room? Write down what works and doesn't work so you can organize your goals for the space.

Maybe you don't have a whole room to dedicate to an office room. Is there an area in your living room, family room, or guest room that could become your home office nook?

What zones do you need to have in your office area? Just a desk area for a computer and printer, or do you also need a crafting area or work island so you can spread out?

Do the kids need to use this space too, or is just for you?

How do you like to work, standing up or sitting down? Do you like to spread your stuff out, or do you prefer a single desk with storage that puts everything at your fingertips?

What sort of technology to you need? A desktop computer with a large monitor? A laptop? What sort of printer do you need? Do you need a fax machine? Do you need a separate phone line or can you use your cell phone? If you are a crafter or artist, do you like having lots of supplies within reach?

What are the simple things you could change now with your current setup? Paint on the walls to bring in your favorite color? If you have wood floors, new area rugs can change the look and feel of the space. Do you have to rip up the carpet to reveal wood floors? Can you add a new window or a larger one to take in a great view and to allow more light in? Can you take that old kitchen table stored in your garage and make it a usable desk? Think about what you already have and how you can use it.

Do you need to buy office furniture, or can you be creative with things? For example, file cabinets topped with a piece of solid wood make a great work surface (paint or stain it). Even sawhorse bases topped with a piece of glass equal an instant desk. Just be sure the desk surface is high enough for you to work at your computer comfortably without neck or back strain. Creative repurposing saves you money and gives you an office with character.

What are other simple things that can change the feel of your present area? New lighting to make it warmer, artwork, favorite books, music, a comfortable seating area, gaining a view to the garden by repositioning your desk?

What kind of theme would you like in your home office? A modern loft setting in black and white? A Parisian artist's space? Southwestern style? Maybe showing off a collection you have?

If you are going to paint, what about doing wide horizontal stripes? What about a dark color on one wall? How about a whole wall of chalkboard paint? You could write out all your random thoughts!

Have you seen any home offices in the movies you have loved? It might be worth looking into for inspiration. Note Diane Keaton's desk in *Something's Gotta Give:* great big desk, organized paperwork, and a nice view. Perhaps the more modern, well-organized home office Liam Neeson had in *Love Actually* is more your taste. See what might make you work at your best, then create that space.

chapter 10

Kids' Spaces

I firmly believe that kids, especially today, need a place to just be kids—to draw, paint, or have uninterrupted time to themselves. As a kid I loved drawing and I had great art teachers who supported my creative pursuits, but creativity starts at home in the spaces children can call their own.

Providing your kids with a space to be creative as well as a room that makes them feel safe and comfortable gives them an important foundation. It does not have to contain much, and it can be very simple in design. The important thing is to create a good environment for them.

For babies, the nursery room is usually simple and furnished with what is necessary—the crib, a changing table, a rocker, some soft toys, and a few books. As kids grow up, the room becomes more about their interests. With the boys in our house, we have gone from the clean lines of a baby's room to a boy's world, with shelves and surfaces for displaying rocks, cool-looking sticks, baseballs, swords, adventure books and still more adventure books, science experiments, and now, something new: taped-up front pages from newspapers heralding the winning World Series team.

It's fun to watch the evolution of your child's room. It may start out reflecting your ideas as a parent, but then they grow up and begin to explore and express their individual personality in their spaces. Teens take their rooms to another level, and making their own design decisions helps them begin to define their style. It's also their responsibility to clean up their room, putting away clothes,

Creativity starts at home in the spaces children can call their own.

and keeping it in order (or not, as the case may be). They might try out new color on their walls, or collage images of who or what they love at the moment. Music and technology become important, and the room becomes a space that feels like an apartment within your home.

As I traveled around shooting homes for this book, I saw many kids' spaces—bedrooms, playrooms, and craft areas—but what resonated with me were the "moments" that gave individual rooms personal style or reflected

*Window seat provides play space with storage below

*A kid's room should express his interests and personality.

*What technology does your teen's room need to accommodate?

*Classic wrought-iron works for a girl's bedroom from pre-teen through college age

what the children loved—the almost thoughtless, casual placement of baseballs or a bunch of toys, things that were placed in the room as if the children were coming right back. Kids' rooms are ever-changing, and you can have a basic plan for their rooms, but there will always be a sense of constantly changing energy and motion to them.

It's important to make classic choices for furniture, to have the basics in place. Invest in pieces that will grow with the child. You can always restyle the accessories and props, but the bed, dresser, bookcase, and desk should be able to take them through the years, from toddler to teen. You can even buy a crib that transforms into a toddler bed and then into a regular bed. I like the idea that a child can come home from college and find her room just the way she left it.

With the main furnishings in place, the next layer is color, which is key for kids. For health and safety, use paints that are low in volatile organic compounds (VOCs)—they give off almost no fumes or odor. Colors that can work as

*A clothesline strung along the wall is great for a changing art display

Invest in pieces that will grow with the child.

*Freshen secondhand furniture with semi-gloss latex paint for a washable surface

your child grows are a good backdrop for a room that will go from playroom to tween/teen hangout over time. A washable finish is essential, especially for a younger child's room. A pearl or eggshell finish stands up to scrubbing but won't show wall defects the way semigloss or high-gloss finishes will. (Save the glossy sheens for trim and moldings.)

Catalogs from mail-order furniture companies are a great source of ideas for children's rooms. They show how to pull together everything you need, from beds to well-designed storage options, lighting, area rugs, window treatments, and even color palettes. But be careful not to make your child's room a "cookie cutter" catalog room. Put up their artwork, family photos, collections—things that reflect their personality and bring the room to life.

As you look at your own children's space, decide what activities the room needs to accommodate. Does the bedroom need to double as their playroom? If so, you'll need to define a sleeping area, dresser/clothes area, reading area, and play area with storage for toys. If the play space is in your family room, maybe you can designate a corner that is theirs for playing, with a table and chairs and storage baskets or shelves for toys and games.

*Insert cork or fabric-covered foamcore in a frame for pinning up cards or photos

*New bedding can change the look or theme as your child grows

Create an Imagination Space

This playroom was originally a family room that was more of a catch-all space, which just happened to have a crafting and play area for the two girls. By looking at it from a different perspective, I saw that most of the items stored there could be removed. That alone would open up the possibilities for the room to become a major imagination space for kids and grownups alike.

To bring the room to life, I defined zones: one for crafting and art projects, another for homework, another for reading and hanging out, and—my favorite part—the stage area for performances and dancing. Although this is a fairly large playroom, you could achieve something similar in an extra bedroom, finished attic, or basement. It could even be adapted to fit into the child's bedroom. The curtains and wire system that define the stage area could double as a way to divide a sleeping area from a storage area of cubbies full of toys or art supplies.

The other thing I liked about this room was that the vibrant wall colors captured a happy mood. To create a sense of greater height in the room, I installed a chair rail higher than usual on the wall, and painted the lower part of the wall green and the upper walls and ceiling blue. This simple visual trick makes the room seem much bigger. Adding a cap molding to the top of the chair rail created a narrow shelf so framed artwork can rest on it. This is a great way to display artwork without putting nails in the walls.

I designated one area for a chalkboard wall for drawing. Paint stores sell chalkboard paint that lets you turn any surface into a blackboard. You could do this in your kid's bedroom, bathroom, or playroom. It's also perfect for a message board in the kitchen or mudroom.

*Built-in storage keeps toys and games organized

*Child-size table for crafts and homework

IDEAS
you can look for and use

It's easy to do a chalkboard wall area yourself with chalkboard paint. Do you have a blank wall space to create your own? Even the back of a door will work.

Don't have a whole piece of furniture for storage of arts and crafts supplies? What about converting a closet for all that good stuff? Or try draping off an area with a decorative fabric panel to conceal the storage.

Can you create your own stage area like this one? It can serve as a room divider if your children share a space, and it's a great way to give them a performance area.

Do you have a corner where you and your kids can take some family time and read together?

Open storage for smaller items is sometimes easier to maintain than closed storage. Store pencils and pens in open baskets or containers, where they're easy to find and look nice out in the open.

You don't have to have a mural that overpowers the room. What about a simple outline or use of color, as in this room?

Use wood trim creatively. You can create a two-tone effect on the walls in your space by dividing up the areas with trim pieces. In the top photo on the left, a narrow shelf at the top was used for display, but you could also separate two wall colors with a strip of lattice or chair-rail molding.

Part of the magic of this space is its use of lighting. Spotlights focus on the stage, and each zone has appropriate lighting, too, for crafting or reading.

Include a big table for craft projects, snacks, and after-school gatherings. Maybe your old kitchen table gets repurposed with some new paint, or you could use a large coffee table with beanbags for chairs.

Soft pillows and a big area rug can make an instant area for hanging out or playing around, yet can be cleared away easily when the need to run and dance takes hold.

Display your kids' artwork! You can use a retractable clothesline and simply use clothespins to hang up their paintings. It's also a great way to dry wet projects, and you can then create backdrops for their shows on stage.

Don't have space for an entire playroom like this? Be creative with a corner of your children's room. You don't need much furniture—keep it to basics, and the space may just give you more possibilities for an imagination space.

Spend some time together in there as a family—you're allowed to play, too!

*Don't forget spotlights!

Accessories and More

Accessories bring the bedroom to life, and letting your kids help with the choices gives them a chance to express themselves and make the room their own. Bedding, table lamps, desk lamps, and artwork can introduce a theme and reinforce the color scheme. Anything can be a starting point for decorating: a vintage collection of toy cars, an old dollhouse from your own childhood, a favorite sport or team, a favorite book or TV show. You can set the stage with the basic backdrop and plan, but your kids' interests bring it life and detail. One word of caution about decorating kids' rooms with vintage toys or furniture: Anything painted before 1978 could have lead-based paint, which is toxic if paint flakes are consumed or paint dust is inhaled. It's best to keep anything that might have lead-based paint on it out of the reach of children.

Toys are obviously going to take center stage for a few years in children's areas, so storage is key. Wherever their play area is, be sure to provide storage that's easy and fun for them to use. If you don't have built-in cabinets, consider a storage cubby with baskets. Label each basket with the types of toys to be stored in it (this makes for easier cleanup time). If they have a lot of books, include a bookcase in the bedroom for quiet-time reading. If you have a crafting area, think about storage for arts and crafts supplies as well as access to a sink for easy wash-up.

Decorating a kid's room can be simple. The details that they will bring to it, with their varied interests and adventurous ways of thinking, will make the room complete. All you need to do is supply the foundation, and they can take it from there creatively!

*Introduce a theme with artwork and bedding.

*A wall unit of cubbies with baskets stores toys or clothes

*A bookcase holds toys now—books later

HOW
to begin?

When planning a child's room, ask yourself these questions:

Will your child's room be a sleeping bedroom only or will it be a playroom, too?

Would it make it easier for you to design around a theme as you put the room together—baseball, flowers, farm, etc.? Your Look Book is a good place to collect fun themes that appeal to you for younger children. Older children and teens can assemble their own Look Books to guide the decorating process.

Does the room need to be painted? If you want to add a splash of color without painting the whole room, could you paint a single wall or just the area behind the bed?

Do you need to buy all new furniture for a child's room? Are there pieces you already have that could be repurposed, such as dressers or nightstands from other rooms in your house? Could you prime and paint them a vibrant color and put on whimsical hardware to make them feel new for your child?

Have you considered buying furniture that will grow with the kids so you don't have to buy new pieces at each phase of their needs?

Are your younger kids getting all the hand-me-downs from the older kids? If so, be sure to freshen the look with paint, new hardware, and new accessories to make them reflect your younger child's style.

What key pieces do you need in the space—bed, nightstand, a comfy chair for reading with them, armoire, etc.? You don't need to buy everything at once, and your child's needs will guide you.

How much toy storage do you need? Could you store some toys in your basement or attic and switch the toys around every so often to avoid having all the toys out all the time? Remember, kids seem to love something one week and then forget about it the next week.

Do you want to control levels of lighting for reading and quiet time, yet have ample light for projects and playtime?

If you have hardwood floors, do you want to add area rugs to soften the room and make things a little quieter, too? Rugs also add color and style to a room. If you have carpeting, layer rugs over areas where kids play often to protect the carpet from wear and staining. If you have the space—such as a finished attic or basement—thick rubber matting for tumbling makes a great playroom-floor surface.

What kind of window treatments do you need? In children's bedrooms, it's important to have light-blocking window treatments, especially for nap times and nighttime. Lined Roman shades are a good choice for any age and either gender. Just remember to tie up the cords so infants and toddlers can't reach them. Draperies add softness and color and can be paired with shades to ensure light control.

For play area storage, will your children put things away in cubbies, or do they need bins that they can pick up and move around? Do they need a play table to spread out their toys? Or is a large area rug sufficient for their playtime?

For older kids, do you mind if they tape things to the walls? If so, how about letting them have one wall—their vision board wall—where they can collage images and things they love from photos, award ribbons, ticket stubs, and so on? Use a reusable puttylike adhesive such as Blu-Tack to attach items without damaging the wall, or paint the wall with magnetic paint and use magnets to hold posters and photos in place.

Music is key in kids' spaces. A CD player tucked on a bookshelf is handy for young children if they go to sleep more easily listening to music. And it's a good trick to use fun music as part of cleanup time for the little ones.

My Favorite Resources

When I do a makeover or client design project, I tend to shop at the same places where you shop. Over the years I have found it is easier to go with what is available in the online sources we all have access to and the everyday stores we can all find. Plus, when I'm on location for a project or shoot, I don't usually have the luxury of lots of time, so I need to locate items within that city quickly. Many times I'm in a location I've never been to before, and finding familiar sources makes my life easier.

Because many of the things that I buy for a project are the final touches, such as smaller pieces of furniture, wall art, lighting, bedding, window treatments, and other props, part of the fun for me is seeing what is available right there at the store. I can check vendor Web sites to get a sense of what stores may have at the moment, but I also allow myself to be inspired when I'm in the store. Based on experience, I know that things will come together the way they should, so I don't stress out over what might or might not be available. Sometimes if something I had in mind isn't available, it is actually for the best because it encourages me to shift focus and be open to other options. That is what it means to be creative on your feet.

There have been many times when I wanted eight panels of curtains in a certain color but could only find six.

Because I can't wait for a special order, I usually have to make a decision right there: Do I forget that color of drapery and find another, or do I stop and reconsider the window treatment altogether? Is there something even better that I had not thought of before? In your home design projects, you probably won't be under that kind of time pressure, but you may find that something you really wanted is no longer available; if so, consider it an opportunity to discover something even better.

Since I am a visual person, I find it useful to visit Web sites and get a sense of what companies are producing and how they interpret what homeowners want and how they live. Some Web sites even include lifestyle videos and slide shows. These showcase their furniture or other products in room settings or in actual homes. You can use these as inspiration, printing out images you love and pasting them into your Look Book. Use them for creative direction, but remember to make them your own, too. It's your own home style.

Here are a few resources that I like and Web sites I enjoy for home, entertaining, and everyday-living ideas. I shop for products at some of these; I use others for inspiration. Check them out.

To see home furnishing products and ideas, I usually go to Web sites such as www.sundancecatalog.com, which is

one of my favorites because it is close to my own personal style. I also go to www.potterybarn.com, www.pbteen.com, and www.pbkids.com because I like how they put rooms together and you can really get a sense of the bigger lifestyle picture. Another fun Web site and a great example of a family-owned business is www.russellmackenna.com. I often like to look at www.westelm.com, www.restorationhardware.com, www.ikea.com, and www.rhbabyandchild.com.

A great place to look at various styles and see what might be to your liking is www.ethanallen.com, and www.zgallerie.com also makes it easy to shop and see what style might be right for each homeowner. I return to these Web sites often, and I like to cut images from their catalogs for future reference or for my vision board of ideas. I also enjoy checking out www.shabbychic.com and www.montauksofa.com for further inspiration and style ideas.

When I'm on the road and looking for props and accessories, World Market (www.worldmarket.com) is a great source for things to finish off a room. For ordering online, I like www.ballarddesigns.com for home accessories and furnishings; www.christmastreeshops.com, a retail chain in some parts of the country, is also a good source. Wonderful bedding is offered at www.pineconehill.com, and www.dashandalbert.com has great carpeting options.

For paint, flooring, or products such as windows and doors, I visit www.benjaminmoore.com, www.mythicpaint.com, www.americanclay.com, www.flor.com, www.harveywindows.com, and www.mannington.com. It's handy to see the various products that are available in one place, plus I get a sense of what's new in the marketplace. For appliances and fixtures, I look at www.whirlpool.com, www.kohler.com, and www.waterworks.com. For cabinets, I look to www.plainfancycabinetry.com and www.omegacabinets.com. I also enjoy outdoor living catalogs and Web sites such as www.gardeners.com and www.smithandhawken.com. Of course, www.lowes.com and www.homedepot.com are places I know I can always find what I need for big and small renovation projects, plus for my own everyday to-do list.

I really love the world of style that Ralph Lauren has created. His Web site (www.ralphlauren.com) has great visual inspiration for fashion as well as the home. The RL

TV section has great lifestyle videos that are very cinematic and convey the idea or mood of various styles.

I wish I had more time to paint, but I do not have as much time as I would like so I'm always looking at what other artists are doing. I urge you to support local artists and talents in your own community, too. John Singer Sargent is my favorite artist, but I am also drawn to artists who capture the use of light and mood the way he did. Check out www.wendyejames.com, www.jonmacadam.com, www.kmmstudio.com, www.rodney-white.com, and www.joanpalanociolfi.com—these are some of my favorite artists on the scene today.

I like to cook, so going online to look up a new recipe idea for Thanksgiving, a special dinner, or even just a quick weekday meal usually takes me to www.barefootcontessa.com, www.marthastewart.com, www.bhg.com, www.jamieoliver.com, and www.rachaelray.com.

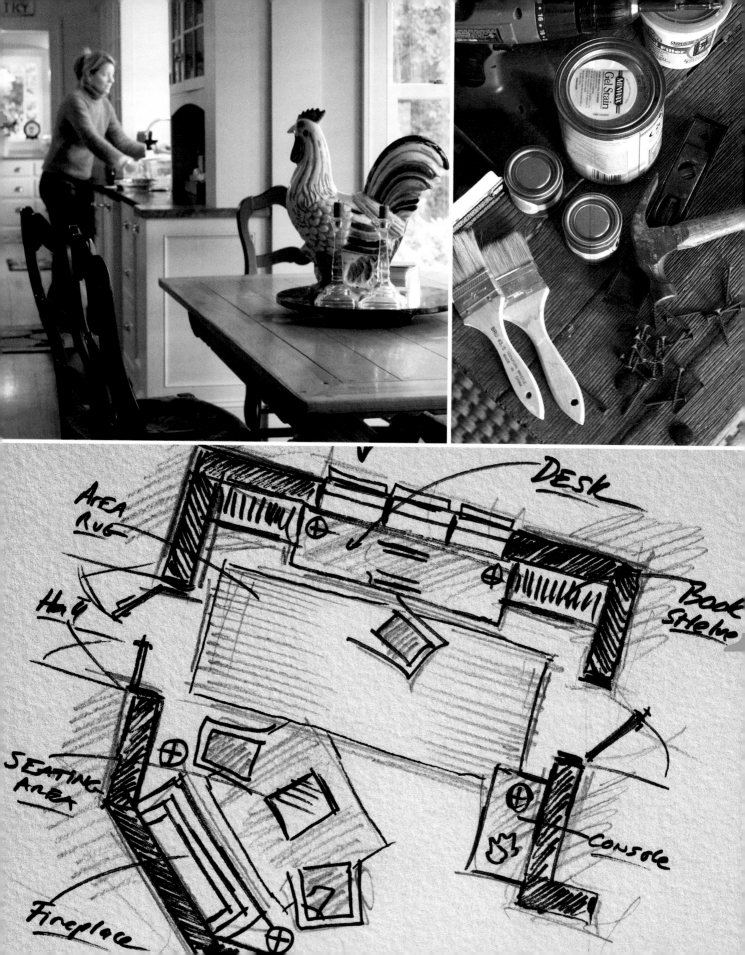

In the End . . .

My goal for this book has been to convey to you that design is not something to be afraid of or confused about. I want you to be motivated and empowered. To achieve that, I've tried to show you how I look at spaces, hoping that will help you see your own home in a different light.

Learning to follow your instincts about design will bring your home to life in the way it deserves and in a way that feels right to you. Your home should be good to you when you walk in the door at the end of the day. You should love being there, and it should be the good foundation of your life, whether you are living in your dream house, in a starter home, or in a small fifth-floor walk-up in the city somewhere. I have seen firsthand how home affects each and every one of us—even in simple ways. If we are surrounded by things that make us happy, that will affect our mood and mindset. If we are beginning to define our style and develop it ourselves, that confidence we gain will give back more to us than we can imagine. Good home design can change your life.

I believe the time has come for a return to excellence in our expectations of ourselves and what we put out there. It's time to refocus on enjoying the simple things in life—taking time out for friends, spending good time with family, and enjoying home again. Each of us has something to share, and I urge you to share it. I hope that what I've brought to this creative table will help you make your home better—and that as a result, you and your family will live a well-rounded, happy, and beautiful life. Wherever you go, you'll know that at the end of your driveway, home is there waiting for you. There truly is no place like home.

Be Creative,

Acknowledgments

I am a firm believer that things happen for a reason. A fork in the road leads us to choices, and we must look toward the path we think is right and move confidently in that direction. Sometimes there are people who come into our lives to help us see which way to go, guide us, remind us of what we are trying to do or simply to come together to work on projects with a bigger picture in mind.

First off, a huge thank you to Cynthia Kitchel and Pamela Mourouzis at Wiley who were the first ones to truly see and understand what I wanted this book to be. Thank you for your clear vision of it.

This book could not have happened at all without the caring, thoughtful guidance of my editor, Vicki Ingham, who molded my almost stream-of-consciousness rough drafts and helped keep my goals for this book on target.

To the team at Wiley, especially to: Susan Olinsky, Wendy Mount, Donna Wright, Elizabeth Brooks, Tai Blanche for their creative works that brought my words and images to life on the pages of this book. To Amy Sell and Malati Chavali for working with me on the marketing end of this project. Thank you to Gypsy Lovett for taking on the publicity for my first book. Thank you all.

To the families who allowed me to come into their homes to photograph them and to my friends along the way, thank you to the following . . .

The Frisch family and Grandma Marliyn, the Lippman family, the Halperin family, the O'Hara family, the Howard family and friends, the Owens family, the Carpenter family, the Sandy family, the Burt family, the Fredericks family, the Pudvar family, the LaBrecque family, the Sudbay family, the Porter family, the Lowe family, the Stratmann family, the Cataldo family, the Wallace/Grant family; special thanks to Peter for all you have done; the Brook/Jemmett family, the Catucci family, the Lindenmeyr family, Ali White, Anne Altern, Maree Gaetani, Trish Peters, Katie McMahon, Charlie Rini, Frank O'Leary, Mary White, Deborah Durham, Gayle Butler and Andy Sareyan for supporting my creative works; Gregory Kayko, Oma Ford, Joanna Linberg, Charlie Graves, Sherry Chris, Samantha Nestor; Nate Beaman and Justin Bunnel for their own creative works and literally running up mountains; Fionnuala Sherry and Rolf Lovland for being the soundtrack for my life, Eileen McComb, Terry Fassburg, Linda Richman who shares my love of old movies, Mary Mac, "the wise Irish one"; Lane Tynan for all that you have done and still do. To my art teachers—I kept being creative because you were part of the journey. Thank you, thank you.

There are certain people who have come into my life, and I am grateful for them on so many levels. Mrs. Blanchard, although you are no longer here, I wish you could finally come to my house and we could share our old stories again by the fire, but somehow I know you are already here. To Ismail Merchant who gave me chances and opened new doors with his larger-than-life presence. You are truly missed. For James Ivory, I admire all that you have done with your artistic eye; the fact that you have remained true to who you are as an artist is the definition of true success in my book. I am thankful for your support and for your body of work, which truly sets the standard I aspire to. To Ro, who gave me my first chance and Marian McEvoy and Carolyn Sollis for being supportive early on.

Lastly, thank you to my wonderful family, the people who support me and who make my life complete. I am so thankful for my wonderful sons, Declan and Dempsey, who are always surprising me with what they are bringing to the world. You guys will do amazing things in your lives, and I cannot wait to be there with you along the journey. I am constantly overwhelmed with pride. To our dog, cats, and hens, who make us laugh and allow me to feel like a farmer from Vermont.

In the end, there is but one person for whom I did this book, my wife, Mary. You get me like no one else ever has, and the journey we've been on has been amazing. We have traveled and reached places we never thought we would find ourselves. We've talked and shared dreams on those quiet nights by the fire. Your spirit is beyond this place and there would be no place like home without you.

Index